VOL. I October, MDCCCCI NO. 1

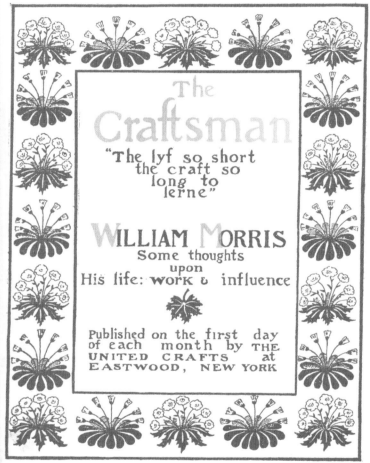

The
Craftsman

"The lyf so short
the craft so
long to
lerne"

WILLIAM MORRIS
Some thoughts
upon
His life: work & influence

Published on the first day
of each month by THE
UNITED CRAFTS at
EASTWOOD, NEW YORK

Price 20 cents the copy

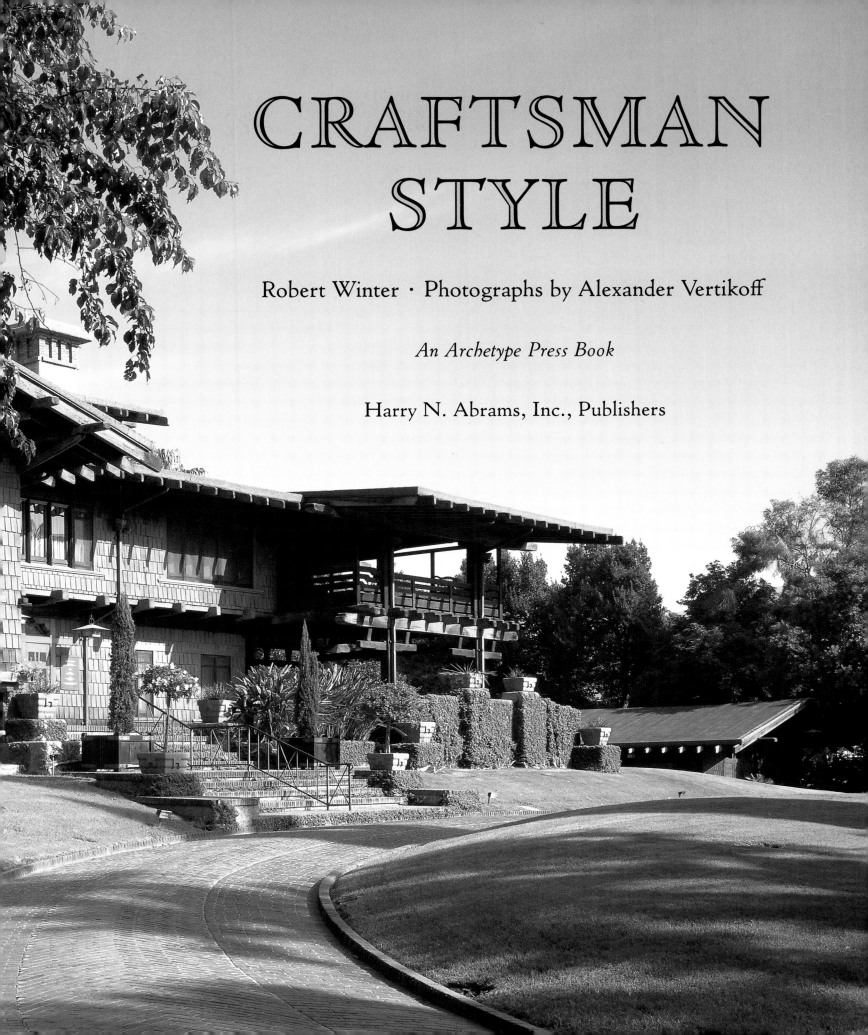

CRAFTSMAN STYLE

Robert Winter · Photographs by Alexander Vertikoff

An Archetype Press Book

Harry N. Abrams, Inc., Publishers

CONTENTS

INTRODUCTION

Printer, poet, socialist, preservationist, furniture maker, wallpaper designer, art glass fabricator, cloth maker—William Morris (1834–96) is generally considered to be the father of the Arts and Crafts movement in Britain. He holds a similar position in the United States, where his disciple, Gustav Stickley (1858–1942), spread Morris's ideas throughout the country in a journal named *The Craftsman*. Published from 1901 to 1916, the publication eventually gave its name to the American movement. For Americans disoriented by the rapid change that the machine had made in their own lives, Morris's critique of modern industrial society spoke strongly to them.

> "Nothing will come of nothing."
> *King Lear,* Shakespeare

His argument came from John Ruskin (1819–1900), whose *Stones of Venice* (1852) Morris had read when he was a student at Oxford. The chapter "The Nature of Gothic" had inspired Morris and his friend Edward Burne-Jones (1833–98) to give up studying for the ministry and to find a different mission in art, Burne-Jones in painting and Morris in architecture. Ruskin's theme was antimodern; the first Renaissance stone laid in Venice was to him the beginning of a downward spiral to materialism and social decay. In contrast stood the presumed organic unity of society in the Middle Ages that made possible the great Gothic cathedrals.

This was a heady brew, but many Americans, even though always a small minority, liked it. William Morris societies and John Ruskin clubs and Arts and Crafts organizations were founded to stimulate discussion of Morris's ideas and to mount exhibitions of handcrafted objects. Most proponents rejected his medievalism, but they could agree with him that industrialization had betrayed its promise of freeing workers from drudgery. They shared his belief that bigness was ruling their lives and wished for "an epoch of rest," the subtitle of his utopian novel *News from Nowhere* (1890). Like him they looked back to a presumably better day before things got out of control.

❦ Opposite. The brothers Charles and Henry Greene have come to epitomize the Craftsman style of woodsy building. At their Gamble House (1908) in Pasadena, California, art glass in the front door transforms the tree of life into an iridescent California oak. It is glorious in the morning.

❦ Below. Sleeping porches such as this one at the Gamble House enticed people back to nature at the turn of the twentieth century, as the Craftsman movement took hold.

It is impossible to study this period without noting the Arts and Crafts movement's resemblance to the exactly contemporaneous Progressive movement in American politics. Both crusades were concerned that individual liberties were being eroded by mechanization, that old values were being lost in the pursuit of materialism, that people were being alienated from the product of their work, and that nature itself was under attack from modernization. Like the Progressives (Stickley was one), the rank and file of craftspeople were conservatives who sought reform by looking backward. Morris is celebrated for his passion to restore the handcraft tradition, at least in his own life. His involvement in so many crafts suggests a symbolic, even therapeutic, interest in denouncing the shoddy factory production of his time, but only indirectly do we get an idea of the kind of architecture he envisioned for a future society free of the profit motive and onerous mechanized work. His novel *News from Nowhere* gives some insight. In his utopia, London would be broken up into small communities separated from each other by forests and gardens. Residential architecture would be blandly pleasing, nothing assertive. When Guest, the narrator, takes his boat trip up the Thames, he finally arrives at an old house described clearly enough so that the reader knows that the model is actually Morris's beloved Kelmscott Manor near Oxford, where he lived intermittently between 1871 and 1875. Built about 1570, it was not medieval but old enough to stand for medieval, Morris's golden age. As Fiona MacCarthy writes in *William Morris: A Life for Our Time* (1995), his sense of history made him a Victorian and not a modernist. "It was his instinct not to jettison but to incorporate the past," she notes.

A much earlier indication of his taste was the house that Philip Webb designed for the Morrises at Bexleyheath, ten miles south of London, in 1859. Remarkably, this Red House gives the same feeling as Kelmscott Manor: age and timeless beauty. Like Kelmscott Manor, it looks older than it is and must have satisfied Morris's medievalism. In fact, Morris liked to think of it as being on the route of Chaucer's pilgrims traveling to Canterbury and named a porch at the rear "Pilgrim's Rest."

❡ Above. The Englishman William Morris was the ultimate craftsman for his age.

❡ Bottom left. Red House (1859, Philip Webb) is the only home Morris ever had built for himself. Like a medieval playhouse, it had lovely details almost everywhere—and well-thought-out spaces for the servants. Its red brick was meant as a gantlet thrown down to lovers of modern stucco.

❡ Bottom right. On the frontispiece of the 1892 edition of Morris's novel *News from Nowhere,* printed by his Kelmscott Press, a drawing of Kelmscott Manor represents the haven at the end of the road. All the typography was designed by Morris.

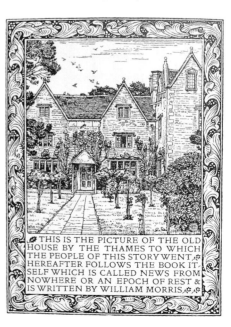

THIS IS THE PICTURE OF THE OLD HOUSE BY THE THAMES TO WHICH THE PEOPLE OF THIS STORY WENT. HEREAFTER FOLLOWS THE BOOK ITSELF WHICH IS CALLED NEWS FROM NOWHERE OR AN EPOCH OF REST & IS WRITTEN BY WILLIAM MORRIS.

¶ Above. Gustav Stickley picked up Morris's torch in the United States, spreading the word in his *Craftsman* magazine as well as in architectural plans, furniture, and household objects sold by catalogue.

¶ Bottom left and right. Beginning in 1904 Stickley published two hundred plans for Craftsman houses, which readers could order for as little as $3. "We have from the first," he declared, "planned houses that are based on the big fundamental principles of honesty, simplicity and usefulness—the kind of houses that children will rejoice all their lives to remember as home."

The pleasant, mellow architecture that Morris envisioned would, he seems to have thought, come after a violent revolution that would clear the air and make the world more reasonable. Here Morris is very vague. We see a leap of faith, an act that is often substituted for hard thought. In spite of his forays into many arts and crafts, Morris did not intend to be a reformer. The change he wanted would follow an apocalypse. His experiments with typography, for example, were done not to inspire others but for his own edification. That his followers actually used his example to reform bookmaking would not have interested him. Similarly, Charles Robert Ashbee (1863–1942), a Morris follower in England who would eventually establish an Arts and Crafts colony at Chipping Campden in the Cotswolds, visited Morris one day in 1887 to tell him of his interest in developing a Guild and School of Handicraft based on the principles of Morris's own business enterprise, Morris and Company. Morris told him that he was wasting time and energy that might be better spent on encouraging a socialist revolution.

Being antimodern ("Apart from a desire to produce beautiful things, the leading passion of my life has been and is hatred of modern civilization," he declared in 1894), Morris avoided endorsement of any contemporary architects. We know what he did not like. When as a youth he was taken to see Sir Joseph Paxton's iron and glass (and wood) Crystal Palace (1849), he refused to go inside. It is no coincidence that when he occasionally spoke of a new building, it was to point out its defects.

Morris's circle of young friends included the architects W. R. Lethaby, Ernest Gimson, Sidney Barnsley, and Detmar Blow, all of them knowledgeable about the English craft tradition and vernacular architecture. All were influenced by Morris's notion of the simple life. Some showed a strong affinity for the Cotswolds, where the architecture was old enough and picturesque enough to be a background for their work. In her biography of Morris, Fiona MacCarthy writes of Detmar Blow's own house:

When he came to build his own house, Hilles in Gloucestershire, it was an idealized version of Kelmscott, a ruralist dream-mansion with stone gables and thatched roof rising steeply above the valley of the Severn. The house was furnished with Morris Sussex chairs and Ernest Gimson settles. It was perhaps the ultimate example of the Simple Life.

FIRST FLOOR PLAN.

American architects would have known very little about these English architects, for they were rarely published in either popular or professional journals. Many would have heard of Lethaby (1857–1931), whose book *Architecture, Mysticism and Myth* (1891) was in many American libraries. Otherwise Morris's inner circle was of little consequence to American architects. Probably they would never have heard of Morris's old friend Philip Webb, the architect of his Red House.

Arts and Crafts architects outside the Morris circle were better known. The work of Charles F. A. Voysey (1857–1941), who denied any connection with Morris but whose houses are closely related in style to those of Morris's architect friends, was featured in a series of articles in the 1899–1900 issues of *International Studio*, a British journal that was republished in the United States with a little American material added. But American architects were rarely influenced by Voysey's exteriors, although they were certainly impressed by his interiors, especially the furnishings that Gustav Stickley, among others, admired.

In *The Craftsman* Stickley was notably short on English subjects, except for a significant number of designs for houses in English garden cities by Barry Parker and Raymond Unwin, who were, like their more talented brethren, celebrants of English vernacular architecture of the sixteenth and seventeenth centuries. Although the garden city idea caught on in places such as Forest Hills Gardens in Queens, New York, Parker and Unwin's stucco walls and high peaked roofs found few adherents among American architects.

The florid designs of M. H. Baillie Scott (1865–1945), an architect who was too late to have been noticed by Morris, were known, if not well known, to American architects. The American graphic designer Will Bradley (1868–1962) was obviously drawn to Scott's work and between November 1901 and August 1902 published articles and his own drawings of interiors in the Scott manner in the *Ladies' Home Journal*. Seeing them, the Pasadena Arts and Crafts architect Charles Sumner Greene (1868–1957) cut out some of the pictures of interiors and a number of pieces of Bradley's furniture and pasted them in his scrapbook, but Greene's work nowhere shows a sign of debt to Scott or Bradley. However, Greene did know the design principles of the Scottish architect Charles Rennie Mackintosh (1868–1928) through articles in *The Craftsman* by Harvey Ellis (1852–1904), a furniture designer for Gustav Stickley's United Crafts. Ellis adopted Mackintosh's manner in drawings for an ideal city house published in *The Craftsman* in 1905, but these were without progeny except for Greene's interiors and possibly the interiors of some houses designed by Irving Gill (1870–1936) in San Diego.

A very large exception to the observation that American Craftsman styles owed little to British precedent is what the architectural historian Vincent Scully has named the Shingle Style, derived from the Queen Anne style of Richard Norman Shaw (1831–1912), one of the greatest of the mid-nineteenth-century English architects. A creator of country houses and urban mansions, he, like Morris and his friends, drew on the English vernacular architecture of the sixteenth and seventeenth centuries, substituting flat tiles for thatch on roofs and using tiles decoratively on the flat surfaces of walls, a practice that had nothing to do with Queen Anne.

As interpreted by American architects such as H. H. Richardson (1838–86) and McKim, Mead and White, the style was Americanized by substituting shingles for

❦ Opposite, top. Arden, Delaware, launched in 1900, was one of the utopian American communities inspired by English garden cities and their Arts and Crafts principles. This stile, proclaiming that "You are welcome hither" (from Shakespeare's *King Lear),* marks a footpath connecting homes with artisans' workshops.

❦ Opposite, bottom. English cottage and Tudor designs, some created by the Philadelphia architect Will Price, link Arden to its English antecedents. The Burgage (1913) sits picturesquely by the aptly named Sherwood Forest, another nod to the great English playwright.

tiles. Their practice coincided nicely with a colonial revival brought on by many factors, including the centennial of the Declaration of Independence and the exposition celebrating it held in Philadelphia in 1876. American architects looked back to the colonial past and found a domestic architecture sheathed in wooden shingles or clapboard. It may be significant that they took their ideas from New England architecture, for at first the legacy of the mid-Atlantic and southern colonies was ignored.

Leland M. Roth has told this story in *Shingle Styles* (1999), a book in this series. It is not by chance that among the architects he includes Frank Lloyd Wright, Ernest Coxhead, A. C. Schweinfurth, Bernard Maybeck, Charles and Henry Greene, Purcell and Elmslie, and Julia Morgan, designers usually associated with the American Arts and Crafts (Craftsman) movement. Their work comes directly out of the earlier architecture of Richardson, McKim, Mead and White, and also Wilson Eyre and William Ralph Emerson. The Shingle and Craftsman styles merge almost imperceptibly.

❦ Below left. Elbert Hubbard brought Morris's ideas to East Aurora, New York, in 1896, when he founded the Roycroft Colony. His press aimed to emulate the master's work, sometimes with a dose of levity.

❦ Below center. Another would-be Morrisite community established by enthusiastic Americans was Byrdcliffe, begun in 1902 in Woodstock, New York. Its Shaker-like furniture, laced with nature motifs in bas-relief panels, was the colonists' most distinctive product. This desk, by Zulma Steele, is dated 1904, like most Byrdcliffe furniture.

❦ Below right. Artus Van Briggle combined a love of sinuous Art Nouveau lines with experimental matte glazes to make his award-winning pottery, which shows the Craftsman fondness for natural surfaces. He called this vase "Lorelei" (1898).

Then what is the difference between the Shingle and Craftsman aesthetic? Time period, of course. The Queen Anne and Shingle styles had pretty much run their course by 1890. Craftsman architecture picked up in the 1890s and then faded away in the early 1920s. Although at first the Shingle Style was applied to the mansions of the rich, Craftsman was usually more middle class—simpler. *Craftsman* was a term that could be used for a two-story house or even a California bungalow, with its unusual mix of Japanese and Swiss details. Despite its Queen Anne roots, a Craftsman house would not be mistaken for a Queen Anne cottage.

Most of the other styles collected under the Craftsman rubric have in common the same beginning and ending dates, roughly 1895 and 1920. The Mission style of Florida and the Southwest and the Prairie style, with its base in the Midwest, also flourished in the twentieth century's first two decades and then all but disappeared. By 1920 only the Americanized Tudor style and the California bungalow, much watered down, remained to march alongside the period revivals that were so popular in the era after World War I.

Several Craftsman design principles also fit together fairly well. The most important is an expression of horizontality. Even in the Mission style, with its towers, the main exterior volumes reveal low-ceilinged interiors and horizontal rows of windows, arches, and pergolas. These were intended to make houses seem to hug the ground as if they had grown from it. Frank Lloyd Wright (1867–1959) was famously explicit on this point in his insistence that in the Midwest houses should reflect the prairie on which they were built, going so far as to suggest that in hilly areas they should be sited on the brow, not the top, of a hill. Indeed, many Craftsman enthusiasts advised "building with nature" so that architecture blended with the scenery—a far cry from most of the preceding Victorian styles. The use of wood shingles and clapboard, already present in the earlier Shingle Style, was now given an ideological base as a complement to nature.

Wood paneling inside, also characteristic of Shingle Style interiors, had its own reason for being. Craftsman interiors were usually dark, sometimes very dark; even artificial lighting barely broke the gloom. But a fire in the fireplace—and almost all Craftsman houses had fireplaces as well as central heating—would gladden the heart of the "gentleman of the house," who, coming home from a hard day's work, could put on his slippers and enjoy the coziness of the place. His wife, "the little lady," would, of course, go to her kitchen (factory!), which was painted white and equipped with the latest gadgets, and fix his dinner.

❆ Above. Charles Greene (top) was the designer and dreamer, while his brother, Henry (bottom), tended more to the business of their Pasadena architecture firm.

❆ Opposite, top. By the time Greene and Greene finished work on the Duncan-Irwin House between 1903 and 1906, the original foursquare residence had been wrapped with a Craftsman masterpiece.

❆ Opposite, center. The English architect C. R. Ashbee observed of Charles Greene that "the spell of Japan is on him." Greene and Greene's Blacker House (1907) clearly evokes the Eastern temples and gardens that so influenced their work. However, the brothers never traveled to Japan but instead absorbed Asia through books.

❆ Opposite, bottom. Greene and Greene houses shared with other Craftsman buildings a tendency to moody interiors. Built in 1904, their Reeve House in Long Beach, California, has survived two moves. The small, two-story house pivots around the cozy brick fireplace for light and warmth. A built-in bench by the hearth made the inglenook that much more inviting.

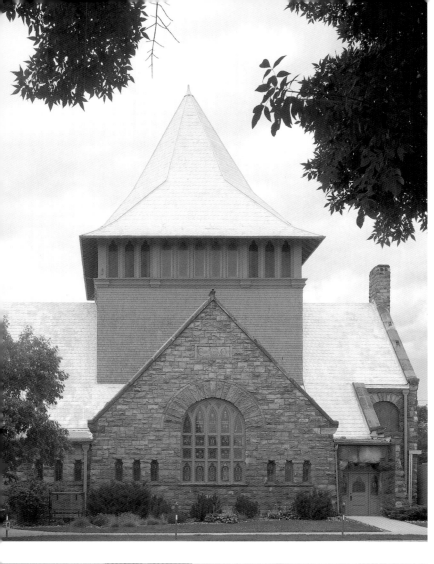

❡ Opposite, top left. H. H. Richardson's rustication of the Romanesque style got Americans interested in buildings with a craftsmanlike air. One of many imitators was the First Congregational Church (1889, Henry Rutgers Marshall, with Robert S. Roeschlaub and Joseph Dozier) in Colorado Springs, Colorado.

❡ Opposite, top right. Its massive rhyolite columns and general solidity of construction show the design's debt to Richardson, although he never attempted a huge witch's-hat tower like the one topping this church.

❡ Opposite, bottom left. The lantern in the witch's-hat tower is an Arts and Crafts interpretation of late Gothic beamed ceilings. This is probably one of the most excited displays of woodwork in any American church.

❡ Opposite, bottom right. The church's Richardsonian exterior cloaks a rich Craftsman interior, including original oak pews and woodwork. Round, arched, and clerestory windows light the sanctuary.

❡ Below. Charles Fletcher Lummis (center) built his love for the old Indian missions into his own Los Angeles home, El Alisal, begun in 1895—complete with a bell tower. After the historic Mission San Juan Capistrano was restored, Lummis paid a visit about 1900.

With the Mission style another sentimental allusion occurred. Like the Shingle Style, Mission Revival buildings looked to the past, in this case to the supposedly simpler and happier period of Spanish occupation of parts of North America. Their source was Helen Hunt Jackson's novel *Ramona* (1884), with its popular portrayal of California's golden age. Jackson was deeply interested in changing government policy toward American Indians. In a mix of fact and fiction, she pictured the nineteenth-century Yankee as the disrupter of an idyllic relationship between the Spanish civilizers and Indians eager for a better life, obviously playing on Yankee guilt, including her own. The novel changed American policy, but, paralleling William Morris's medieval ideal, it also reinforced nostalgia for a better day.

Charles Fletcher Lummis (1859–1928), a Harvard man who built his own Craftsman domicile in Highland Park, a suburb of Los Angeles, saw the beauty of Jackson's myth and set out to save what was left of the Spanish and Indian cultures. He founded the California Landmarks Club in 1894 to preserve the Spanish missions and at the same time devoted much time to collecting Indian artifacts and recording their songs on Edison phonograph cylinders. One result was the Southwest Museum (1910–14), which houses a great collection of American Indian art in a Mission Revival structure.

It would seem that this cultural nostalgia, even if based on myth, was behind other Craftsman styles as well. Surely there is some significance in the fact that Tudor, for example, spoke for the greatest period in English history, the age of Queen Elizabeth I and William Shakespeare. Similarly, Gustav Stickley's decision to employ the log cabin for his community hall (later his home) at Craftsman Farms (1910) in New Jersey celebrated a bucolic day before cities, when humans faced nature squarely.

The 1890 census had suggested that America was fully settled, that its frontier was gone. At an 1893 meeting of the American Historical Association on the grounds of the World's Columbian Exposition in Chicago, Frederick Jackson Turner gave his famous "Frontier Hypothesis" address, in which he raised the question of what would happen now that America's westward movement had supposedly ceased. It is tempting to suggest that the response to this self-scrutiny was the creation of national parks in which inns and outbuildings would favor nature with walls of rough-hewn logs and rustic-looking Craftsman furniture set in front of huge boulder fireplaces.

Going still deeper into the American past, Mary Elizabeth Jane Colter (1869–1958) invented a picturesque pseudo–American Indian style for her buildings at the Grand Canyon and elsewhere. Frank Lloyd Wright and Greene and Greene turned to Asia and applied their notions of Japanese aesthetics to their escapes from the present. Probably unaware that he was contributing to modernist ideas, Irving Gill pared away the Mission style to its geometrical essentials but wrote an article for one of the last issues of *The Craftsman*, obviously associating himself with its conservative stance.

25

Although the Craftsman movement never really died out in the 1920s, it certainly was not a major force in the 1930s, 1940s, or 1950s. Then suddenly in the 1960s it reappeared. Renewed interest began with its architecture. Jean Murray Bangs, the wife of the architect Harwell Hamilton Harris, rediscovered Charles and Henry Greene in her October 1948 article "Greene and Greene" in *Architectural Forum*. Then Esther McCoy, in *Five California Architects* (1960), reintroduced Bernard Maybeck (1862–1957), and Randell Makinson further illuminated the Greenes' work. The most important rediscovery was the architecture of Frank Lloyd Wright, who appeared on Mike Wallace's television show in the 1950s and whose Fallingwater (1935) in Pennsylvania became a national treasure through the publication of magnificent photographs. H. Allen Brooks's work on designers influenced by Wright, *The Prairie School,* was published in 1972, and in 1983 Richard Longstreth's book *On the Edge of the World* showcased Willis Polk, Ernest Coxhead, A. C. Schweinfurth, and other San Francisco Bay Area architects. The first major recognition of this Craftsman revival was a 1972 exhibition of Arts and Crafts artifacts at Princeton University, organized by Robert Judson Clark. Since then there have been many such exhibitions.

The neo-Craftsman movement appeared at the same time that the postmodern movement came on the scene. The postmodernists, impatient with the "Less is more" aesthetic ("Less is a bore," proclaimed Robert Venturi), branched out into a number of expressive modes, using historic styles plus pop art to play jokes on the modernist International Style. But the Craftsman revival was more serious and less conscious of its role as a critic of modernism. The revival clearly contradicted modernism's antiseptic purity.

26

❦ The English garden city movement gave birth to several planned communities in the United States, an idea with which Americans continue to experiment. Forest Hills Gardens in Queens, New York, was laid out by the eminent landscape architect Frederick Law Olmsted Jr. in 1911, with buildings designed by Grosvenor Atterbury. An almost forgotten masterpiece, it remains today almost exactly as it was planned.

€ Bungalows, including bungalow courts, have led the revival of interest in Craftsman architecture, in part because there are so many of them. Although somewhat ignoring the Craftsman ideal of a single-family home set in its own garden, bungalow courts made stylish dwellings available to a wide range of income groups. Pasadena's Bowen Court (1910, Heineman and Heineman) offered twenty-three gabled bungalows on an L-shaped plot.

Undoubtedly the strongest signs of the revival of the Craftsman movement were the soaring prices of Tiffany lamps and Stickley furniture left over from the earlier movement. In the case of Tiffany, the choice pieces were the highly colorful ones, almost camp in their flamboyance. With the Stickley furniture, it was the fine grain of the oak and the seeming simplicity and excellence of the fabrication that attracted the diligent collector. And, of course, success bred scarcity, with the result that these crafts were reproduced by highly skilled artisans who rivaled their ancestors in workmanship and in the prices they charged for it.

In architecture the picture is brighter. For one thing, the Craftsman architectural tradition was sustained through the period of the International Style. With a few exceptions, the American avant-garde was relatively conservative compared to its European manifestation. Some architectural historians have called this period "soft modernism." American modernists always retained a reverence for Frank Lloyd Wright, even though they did not imitate his work. Richard Neutra (1892–1970) and R. M. Schindler (1887–1953), modernists who were admirers of Wright, erred on the side of expressionism.

As criticism of modernist architecture increased in the 1960s, the Craftsman tradition was revived, especially in California and sometimes within the modernist camp itself. In southern California, Harwell Hamilton Harris (1903–90), who began his career in Neutra's office, consciously turned to the work of Charles and Henry Greene and Frank Lloyd Wright for inspiration. Later, Ray Kappe, Cliff May, and Buff, Straub and Hensman would sustain the woodsy phase of Craftsman architecture.

Arts and Crafts architecture survived best in the San Francisco Bay Area. Its roots in the work of Ernest Coxhead, Bernard Maybeck, John Hudson Thomas, Julia Morgan, Louis Christian Mullgardt, A. C. Schweinfurth, and Henry Gutterson were extensive and deep. Unlike the semidesert conditions of southern California, the lush growth that luxuriated in a climate of fog and rain was a wonderful background for brown shingled houses. Nature was kind. Just as important was the relationship of so many of its Craftsman architects to Berkeley, an aspiring academic community where high thinking was believed to be dependent on simplicity of surroundings, an idea expounded by Charles Keeler in *The Simple Home* (1904).

As in southern California, there was a close connection between the early Craftsman movement and the new one. Building in the Bay Area lagged during the Great Depression and the war years, but the work of William Wurster (1895–1973) bridged this time of economic and political troubles and in fact became more and more Craftsman after World War II. In 1927 Wurster built a wood house for the Gregorys near Santa Cruz but painted it white. In 1949 a house he designed in Woodside was so low and brown that it fitted perfectly into Lawrence Halprin's landscaped garden, itself an improvement on nature.

Wurster and other designers of "natural" houses suggest an alternative to cold "less is more," "machine for living" modernism. These California innovators went to architecture schools that taught the spartan aesthetic of Le Corbusier (1887–1965), Walter Gropius (1883–1969), and Ludwig Mies van der Rohe (1886–1969). They knew the language of modernism and also its great contributions to our way of seeing architecture. Without becoming quaint, they also rejected formalism.

Modern Craftsman architecture has fared best in California, perhaps because the first wave of Craftsman architects included so many gifted ones—or was it because California's historic identification as a retreat from modernism was so deeply a part of its history? Certainly in the last twenty years, the Midwest has produced little serious Craftsman architecture. The East is swarming with Arts and Crafts zealots, but they tend to be craftspeople and not architects. The South has a few good Craftsman buildings from the early twentieth century but no strong tradition of Craftsman architecture. Only Fay Jones, a follower of Frank Lloyd Wright, stands out as an equal of the California folks.

It has been pointed out that the present great interest in the Arts and Crafts has now lasted longer than the original movement. In the case of the artifacts, enthusiasm for the subject comes from the joy in making beautiful things by hand and the delight in seeing these well made. The popularity of Craftsman architecture, both old and new, lies in the fact that it looks like home. I can tell you this because I live in California in a Craftsman house. It is good to come home.

❦ Above. Although Tudoresque, the Dungan House (1911, John Hudson Thomas) in Berkeley, California, has plenty of wood to tie it firmly to the Craftsman tradition. It weaves through large trees and bridges a stream that flows across the property.

❦ Opposite. The home that Ray Kappe designed for himself in Pacific Palisades, California, in 1965 is also a bridge—between the simplicity of the first Bay Area Craftsman houses and the refinement of the modern movement. It fits into its wooded environment as naturally as does the Dungan House from a half century earlier.

SINGULAR
VISIONS

EL ALISAL

I f the Arts and Crafts movement can be seen as a haven for eccentrics—beginning with William Morris, its father—no one measures up better than Charles Fletcher Lummis (1859–1928). After graduating from Harvard he briefly edited a newspaper in Chillicothe, Ohio, and then made a break for the West, offering to walk all the way to California. In return for a job when he reached Los Angeles, Lummis telegraphed stories of his experiences along the way to the *Los Angeles Times*. On September 12, 1884, he set out on a journey that would take him through southern Indiana, Illinois, and Missouri to Kansas, Colorado, New Mexico, and Arizona and on into California.

Charles Fletcher Lummis, with Sumner P. Hunt
1895–1928 · Los Angeles

Lummis brought the Arts and Crafts movement with him. His interest in the Craftsman aesthetic was stimulated by his Harvard professor Charles Eliot Norton, a close friend of John Ruskin and an acquaintance of William Morris who later served as the first president of the Boston Society of Arts and Crafts. Lummis's life in Los Angeles reflected Morris's principles to a remarkable degree, although he never directly acknowledged it. His work in architectural preservation, his interest in folklore, his construction of a home with his own hands and his intention to furnish it with tables and chairs that he designed and made, even his writing of poetry—all suggest a Morris connection.

℄ Right. Massive boulders seem to cascade down the walls of El Alisal, ending in rustic piles that anchor Lummis's house to the earth. Although the north and east sides were stuccoed, they were probably also intended to be covered with boulders.

℄ Below. The iron *rejas* (brand) on the left side of the paired front doors was created by the painter Maynard Dixon (1875–1946), as were the hinges modeled on Incan sculpture.

Lummis's greatest contribution to the American Arts and Crafts movement was opening it to the American Indian and Spanish cultures. Like his friend Theodore Roosevelt, he was a social Darwinist who saw both cultures declining in strength. Lummis's hegira to the West began the same year that Helen Hunt Jackson published *Ramona*, which reinforced his views that modern society was being corrupted by material progress.

Never a modernist, Lummis set out to study and preserve the Indian and Spanish cultures. He became a crusader for Indian education and civil liberties, collected manuscripts from the Spanish period that are now treasures of the Los Angeles Public Library, and founded the California Landmarks Club (1894) to save the Spanish missions, most of them in ruins. For these and other services to Spanish-American understanding, the king of Spain knighted him in 1917.

The house that Lummis began building in 1895 on the banks of the Arroyo Seco, in what is now Highland Park, reflects his ethnographic interests and led Frederick Remington to comment in 1903: "Anyone who can build a house as Lummis has done is as great an artist as any of us." With the help of at least one Indian from the Isleta Pueblo in New Mexico, he hauled boulders from the nearby arroyo to create El Alisal, named after a large

sycamore on the patio. First the two built a superstructure of conventional wood frame and then used the boulders to face the building on the south and west sides. Apparently Lummis's architect was his friend Sumner P. Hunt (1865–1938). In his *Journals* (1901), Lummis mentions blueprints, but the house looks as if it were built to the rule of thumb.

The shapes of the windows vary picturesquely. The dining room facade is a boulder-fronted *companario* based on the bell tower at the San Gabriel Mission. Concrete fireplaces were installed by native labor and decorated in the latest styles. Acoma pots are joined by an autographed picture of the king of Spain framed in burnt wood along with samples of Lummis's "Birtch Bark Poems" and other writings. His personal touch is everywhere.

❦ Above. El Alisal's rugged stone chimney shows evidence that Lummis and his crew used an Indian mortar for the boulders.

❦ Opposite. In a picture window at El Alisal, a central pane of glass is surrounded by lantern slides that depict Indian rites in the Southwest as well as in Central and South America. One's home, said Lummis, "should be enduring and fit to endure. Life and death will hallow it...."

In his *Journals* Lummis wrote eloquently of the house he had built:

A man's home should be part of himself.... It should be good architecture, of honest construction, comfortable, convenient, fire proof, burgler [sic] proof, time proof; a possession, not a task master. Something of the owner's individuality should inform it. Some activity of his head, heart, and hands should make it really his. The more of himself that he can put into it, the better for it and for him—even for purely selfish motives. Everyone knows that the thing he has made is more genuinely his than the thing he has bought. The creative thrill is so fine and keen, it is pitiful for a man to get a home off the bargain counter, and miss all the joy he might just as well have had in building it.

In 1985, at the celebration of the one hundredth anniversary of Lummis's famous walk to California, the Spanish consul in Los Angeles noted that Spanish scholars still draw on his works in writing the history of the Spanish Southwest. A representative of the Navajo people also praised Lummis for his contribution to the welfare of American Indians and his leadership in preserving their culture. His vast store of Indian pottery, baskets, and rugs forms the nucleus of the collections of the Southwest Museum, which Lummis founded in 1907 and Hunt designed for a hill near El Alisal. Lummis even recorded Indian songs on Edison wax cylinders. With the help of President Theodore Roosevelt, he moved the dispossessed Cupeño tribe to the Pala Mission, which he had helped preserve. So deep was his love of Indian lore that his friend Charles Keeler referred to Lummis as "William Morris turned into a Mexican Indian."

❧ Opposite: A built-in seat in El Alisal's living room was designed by the painter Maynard Dixon. Above it the lantern-slide window projects patterned sunlight into the space. Once a virtual museum of southwestern arts and crafts, the room was dubbed El Museo by its owner.

❧ Right. A built-in sideboard in the dining room was also designed by Maynard Dixon. Lummis began to collect American Indian pottery after being introduced to Greek pots at Harvard. Although reluctant to give Harvard credit for anything, he gained an appreciation for the culture of the Southwest from Charles Eliot Norton's famous course in the history of the fine arts.

DUNCAN·IRWIN HOUSE

During the twentieth century the rise and fall and rise again of appreciation for the Pasadena architects Charles Sumner Greene (1868–1957) and Henry Mather Greene (1870–1954) followed the cycle of the Arts and Crafts movement itself. Busy and well published in the first two decades of the twentieth century, the Greenes lost their glamour in the 1920s, the era of period revivals, and were rediscovered only in the 1950s and 1960s, first by Jean Murray Bangs and then by Randell Makinson, who recognized their genius when few other critics and historians did. Needless to say, today they have risen to the status of saints in the Craftsman revival.

Charles and Henry Greene
1901, 1903, 1906
Pasadena, California

The Greenes were both born near Cincinnati, but their lineage was pure New England—Charles Sumner named after the famous senator from Massachusetts during the Civil War period and Henry Mather signaling the Greenes' connections with the great New England divines of the seventeenth and eighteenth centuries. The Greene family moved to St. Louis in 1874, and the boys were enrolled in the Manual Training School at Washington University, Charles in 1884 and Henry the next year.

After the brothers' graduation their father, a medical doctor, apparently sensed his sons' artistic inclinations and encouraged them to pursue careers in architecture. They enrolled at the Massachusetts Institute of Technology as "special students," meaning that they would pursue a two-year curriculum in architecture rather than the usual four-year term. In 1888 the brothers set out for MIT, whose campus was then in downtown Boston near H. H. Richardson's already famous Trinity Episcopal Church (1872–77). They would have something to look at.

❦ Right. The facade of the Duncan-Irwin House is one of Charles and Henry Greene's finest designs. Its expansive picture window takes in the valley of the Arroyo Seco, which Teddy Roosevelt said would make one of the most beautiful parks in the world.

❦ Left. The Greenes were masters of the art of mixing clinker (overfired) brick with boulders from the nearby Arroyo Seco. Used on the chimney, these rustic materials marry the house to the earth on which it stands.

❰ Left. French doors in the Duncan-Irwin House dining room lead into the enclosed patio—unique in the Greenes' work—and through another set of doors to the library. The table and chairs were produced by Gustav Stickley's United Crafts.

❰ Below. The brothers' Bandini House (1903; demolished) in Pasadena ranged around three sides of a court but was much simpler in conception. Here the fully enclosed interior courtyard rises up to bring light into the house's second story.

❦ Opposite. The original dining room has now become the main entrance hall of the Duncan-Irwin House. Its clinker brick fireplace has the roughness Greene and Greene liked in their masonry. On the table to the left of the Stickley bow-arm chair stands an unusual Roycroft "American Beauty" vase.

❦ Below. The Stickley sideboard in the dining room is identical to the one that was here in the Irwins' time. The vase is Jauchen and the lamp Handel. All the other pieces were crafted by the Roycrofters.

The architecture department at MIT had been organized in 1865 by William R. Ware (1832–1913), who had worked in the office of Richard Morris Hunt (1827–95), the first American graduate of the Ecole des Beaux-Arts in Paris. It was natural that the course of study was based on Beaux-Arts principles, including a system of related courses and requirements such as examinations at specified times. Because the time-honored way of training to become an architect had been simply to work as an apprentice (the British called it articled) in a certified architect's office, this more formal training was revolutionary.

Henry, the bookish brother, did well under this system, but Charles, the dreamer who was as interested in painting as in architecture, had problems with it. Both, however, got their certificates in 1891 and went into prominent architecture firms in Boston. Then their parents moved to Pasadena. That fact in addition to the dire economic situation of the early 1890s seems to have influenced them to seek opportunities in the West. In August 1893 they visited the World's Columbian Exposition in Chicago and then proceeded by railroad to Pasadena.

The Greenes' good education helped get them commissions in the growing city. At first they designed modest houses in the variety of styles that were popular at the time, the Shingle Style they had known in the Boston area being one of them. From it they gradually developed their own characteristic style, a kind of merger of Japanese temple architecture with the Swiss chalet—and, of course, shingles.

The Duncan-Irwin House is an early example of that development. The front elevation has Asian details and a Swiss connection and is covered with shingles. The interior, however, is almost without allusion to any historic style, in the manner we usually think of as Craftsman. Much more than the Greenes' famous Gamble, Blacker, Pratt, and Thorsen Houses, it exhibits the simplicity of design that we expect from followers of William Morris. The architects play off linearity against spatial complexity in a way that they would rarely repeat.

❰ Above. This piano case added by the current owners of the Duncan-Irwin House was designed by the British architect M. H. Baillie Scott with doors to hide the keyboard. Compared to most of his productions, it is vastly understated.

❰ Right. The diagonal space stretching from the living room to the dining room resulted from one of the remodelings and was not repeated in any other Greene and Greene designs. In the tiled fireplace, seahorse andirons from Roycroft are paired with a green Rookwood tile on the mantel. The grandfather's clock was fashioned by the Shop of the Crafters in Cincinnati.

⟨ Opposite. The staircase in the Duncan-Irwin House's original front hall is small in size, but the immaculate detail à la Japonaise is marvelous. Each window is a different height in order to fit the stair tread.

⟨ Right. A second-floor balcony surrounds three sides of the courtyard, giving outside access to the bedrooms for a taste of true California indoor-outdoor living.

Some of the effect is due simply to the fact that the original house was given two major additions. It began as a one-and-one-half-story cottage that Katherine Mohn Duncan, a seamstress, moved to a spectacular site overlooking Pasadena's Arroyo Seco in 1901, only about fifty feet from where Charles Greene was building his own house. Duncan had the Greenes add six rooms in 1903 and then in 1906 sold the house to Theodore Irwin, a millionaire from Oswego, New York. With the probable encouragement of his friends, James and Nora Culbertson, who lived in a Greene and Greene house across the street, he had the brothers enlarge the house half again.

By this time the front door had been blocked almost out of sight by new construction, so Irwin asked the Greenes to design another door closer to the street. They obliged by adding a portico and an elaborate pergola on the southwest. The architects took advantage of the magnificent view of the Arroyo Seco by installing large plate glass windows in the living and dining rooms. But the space moves inward as well as outward, leading to the center of the house where, enclosed by shingled walls, a small two-story patio awaits with a fountain.

Although the Greenes' major houses have quite conventional floor plans based on Beaux-Arts rationality, the Duncan-Irwin House is full of surprises every few feet. Its flowing space is almost worthy of Frank Lloyd Wright, and the result is thrilling. The Greenes went on to design much more elaborate houses but none so romantic as this one.

€ Above. Mrs. Irwin's bedroom upstairs has a Grueby tile fireplace in a cheerful blue. Surrounded by Craftsman furniture, Ann Chaves, a textile artist, now uses the space for her needle arts. Another bedroom has been converted into a workroom.

€ Below. Off the children's room, a bathroom (left) is furnished with a tub designed to a child's scale. A built-in settle (right) carries the lighter tones often used for upper stories in Craftsman houses. The wisteria pillow was created by the owner.

€ Opposite. Grueby tile in a Navajo pattern frames the firebox in the master bedroom, but the real eye-catcher here is Greene and Greene's play with vertical space—one of the few instances in which the brothers practiced this principle of design.

RIORDAN MANSION

In Texas, New Mexico, and Arizona—the area of the Spanish conquest of North America—the Craftsman movement was usually expressed through the Mission Revival style. The mission image signaled a nostalgia for an invented past when *caballeros* and *padres* maintained a close relationship with the native peoples they had "civilized." Needless to say, the style represented a simplistic interpretation of a story that was more complex than the myth suggested.

The chief boosters of the mission image, ironically, were the railroads—agents of modernization. The Union Pacific Railway in California and the Santa Fe Railway in the Southwest were also the most consistent of all the capitalistic enterprises in cultivating the romantic belief that a better day had preceded the Yankees' arrival. Almost all of their stations and hotels were in the Mission Revival style, a handy advertising device that fired the imagination of traveler and settler alike. In the Southwest the architect most responsible for these psuedo-mission outposts was Charles Whittlesey.

Charles Whittlesey · 1904
Flagstaff, Arizona

As a young man Whittlesey (1867–1941) moved to Chicago, where he found work in the office of Louis Sullivan (1856–1924). An ornamentalist, the great architect was a profound influence on Whittlesey's work, including Philharmonic Hall (1906; demolished) in downtown Los Angeles and the Viennese Room in the Wentworth Hotel (1906) in Pasadena, now the Ritz-Carlton Huntington.

❦ Below and right. Resembling an oversized log cabin, the Riordan Mansion was actually constructed of planks from local ponderosa pines applied over a wood frame. Parts are shingled. Volcanic rock formed into spacious arches visually ties the house to the ground.

❡ Above. The floral art glass in the window transoms of the Timothy Riordan family's breakfast room is so sophisticated that it raises the question of who made it. Originally it was thought to be by Louis Tiffany.

❡ Left. The same family's dining room is based on an oval with a locally made, canoe-shaped dining table of Douglas fir to match. The *paterfamilias* sat in one of the two tall chairs. The sideboard is curved to fit the room, while arched openings over doors and windows also accent the room's shape.

❉ Above. This workmanlike kitchen in the Riordan Mansion is typical of early-twentieth-century houses. In addition to the iron stove with a hot water tank attached, a cabinet was built in. The useful pass-through streamlined service to the dining room.

❉ Left. Bathrooms in most Craftsman houses have been remodeled. This one is completely intact, down to its "sanitary" white fixtures: a high-tank toilet, a wall-hung sink, and a footed tub. Cabinets were also built in for modern efficiency.

In 1900 Whittlesey became the Santa Fe Railway's chief architect and designed many of its depots and hotels. The Albuquerque, New Mexico, station and nearby Alvarado Hotel (1902; demolished) were his first for the Santa Fe, but many more were built to his designs, sometimes with interior features by Mary Colter. Such a building was the famous El Tovar (1905) on the Grand Canyon's south rim in Arizona. As if to defer to the canyon's beauty or because he knew he could not equal it, Whittlesey designed a building that on the exterior seems nondescript; a Santa Fe brochure, however, noted that it "combined in admirable proportions the Swiss chalet and the Norway villa." The interior was pure Craftsman, with peeled logs and furniture of the austere, solid sort that Gustav Stickley was producing, although it was probably made by Stickley Brothers in Grand Rapids, Michigan. "El Tovar is probably the most expensively constructed and appointed log house in America," asserted a writer for *The Hotel Monthly,*

One year before El Tovar was constructed, the Riordan Mansion (Kinlichi) in Flagstaff, Arizona, was built in the same style. Whittlesey's success with the Santa Fe Railway servicing Flagstaff undoubtedly recommended him to the Riordans, but instead of designing a Mission-style house, he chose the woodsy Swiss chalet—his clients were, after all, in the lumber industry.

Timothy and Michael Riordan, brothers from Chicago, married Caroline and Elizabeth Metz, sisters from Cincinnati, and moved together to Flagstaff to join their older brother Denis Matthew Riordan, who ran a lumber mill there. In 1897 Dennis turned over his shares in the mill to his brothers and went into business elsewhere. Just weeks afterward, the mill burned down, but the determined young entrepreneurs built a larger one in its place and renamed it the Arizona Lumber and Timber Company. Business boomed, and soon the brothers were the largest employers in northern Arizona.

❧ Below. The breakfast room in the Michael Riordan family's half of the house is almost a duplicate of his brother's, but the materials differ slightly. The perforated wainscoting in a tulip pattern mirrors the motifs in the art glass window transoms.

Always close, the Riordans decided to build a house—actually a rather grand duplex—in which both of their families could live. In the Craftsman tradition, Whittlesey took advantage of local materials. For the framing and exterior siding as well as the dark-stained interior woodwork, he used ponderosa pine (Flagstaff is in the middle of the nation's largest ponderosa pine forest). The foundation and chimneys were made of volcanic rock from nearby quarries.

Joined by a hall, called the "cabin" because of its exposed log construction, the two houses have almost identical floor plans. The complex is huge: each wing encompasses six thousand square feet, with the thousand-square-foot cabin, used for common leisure activities, in between. One house has eight bedrooms, the other seven, including servants' quarters. The plan, extraordinary to begin with, has other unusual features such as Timothy Riordan's oval dining room.

Some of the furniture was locally made, but the Riordans were up-to-date. They ordered five Harvey Ellis–designed pieces from Gustav Stickley's United Crafts. Stickley's usual line of furniture was foursquare and sometimes awkward—"the sort of thing," as one male chauvinist dealer once remarked, "that you can throw at your wife and it won't hurt the furniture a bit." Ellis, who was with Stickley only a year (1903–4), changed all this. His elegant furniture has inlaid wood designs that show their debt to Sullivan and also to the Vienna Secessionists. The Riordans, or their advisers, had good taste. They also ecumenically ordered some items from Gustav's brothers L. and J. G. Stickley.

As for Whittlesey, he finally settled in Los Angeles, where he conducted early experiments in the use of reinforced-concrete construction.

❡ Above. What was called the "back porch" served as the Riordans' summer kitchen, complete with built-in and free-standing ice boxes. It was later enclosed.

❡ Opposite. In the rustic "cabin" that links the Riordan Mansion's two halves, plank walls provide a suitable backdrop. The bark-framed window features a transparent image by Jack Hillers printed on glass; it can be seen from the inside in daylight and from the outside at night. A coat hangs on a double coat rack by Gustav Stickley.

FONTHILL

Of all the remarkable Arts and Crafts proponents, Henry Chapman Mercer (1856–1930) is probably the most remarkable. Born into a genteel Victorian family of considerable wealth, he was schooled at private academies and naturally enough went to Harvard, from which he was graduated in 1879. While there he, like Charles Lummis, was influenced by Charles Eliot Norton. Mercer entered the University of Pennsylvania Law School and in 1881 was admitted to the Philadelphia bar. But he never really practiced law—he was too busy traveling.

Henry Chapman Mercer
1908–12
Doylestown, Pennsylvania

Mercer's interest in history led him to Europe, where he also took up archaeology. He remained a student of many subjects that he pursued far beyond an amateur's patience. Cleota Reed notes in *Henry Chapman Mercer and the Moravian Tile Works* (1987) that his career spanned the fields of prehistoric archaeology, museum and exhibition design, folklore and folk songs, American material culture and vernacular architecture, and local history. In his spare time he collected prints, played the fiddle, wrote fiction, and enjoyed the music of Wagner.

❦ Left. Seven terraces gave Henry Mercer expansive views out over his seventy-seven-acre property, which included his Moravian Pottery and Tile Works in addition to Fonthill.

❦ Below. Fonthill's facade is a congeries of disparate forms: zigzagging rooflines, multiple chimneys, a hodgepodge of windows, arches low and tall, projecting balustrades, and red tiles punctuating cool concrete. Walls carry marks from the wooden molds into which the concrete was poured. Surely no other house in America is so picturesque.

59

Exotic Moorish tiles seen in Spain soon enough turned Mercer's eye toward yet another endeavor: tilemaker. Machine-made tiles such as those being manufactured in England and America stood as the antithesis of his Arts and Crafts soul, so he set out to design and handcraft his own. "He had experimented with the red clays that he found in deposits near Doylestown, and corresponded with the great English tilemaker, William de Morgan," notes Reed, "but his immediate inspiration came from his observation that while the Arts and Crafts movement had been successful in pottery, nothing similar had occurred in the production of tiles. His entry into designing and making tiles was intended to be revolutionary and it certainly turned out that way."

Mercer designed three major buildings in the Doylestown area: Fonthill (1908–12), his own house; the Moravian Pottery and Tile Works (1910–12); and a museum for his collection of thirty thousand preindustrial hand tools (1913–16). He claimed that he alone was responsible for their design, but a number of architects moved in his aesthetic circle. Will Price and Hawley McLanahan were friends and used quantities of his tiles in their buildings in Rose Valley and in the Marlborough-Blenheim and Traymore Hotels in Atlantic City, New Jersey. Wilson Eyre (1858–1944), another prominent Philadelphia architect, was a close friend and often talked architecture with Mercer, although there is no evidence that Eyre had anything to do directly with Mercer's buildings. Reed, noting that all three structures were early experiments in reinforced concrete, suggests that in structural matters Mercer had plenty of advice from Robert Leslie, editor of *Cement Age* magazine. She also points out that Mercer's acquaintance George Elkins was a director of the Vulcanite Cement Company and that Doylestown is not far from Portland, Pennsylvania, one of the great producers of cement.

For Fonthill, Mercer himself provides a good description of his intentions and method of design:

Several sketches and memoranda in my notebooks show that the building of "Fonthill" was first considered definitely during my visit to New England in the summer of 1907, and that the cheerful confronting of certain houses, overlooking Commercial Street, Boston, were studied for this purpose.

⁌ Above. "Spanish Border" tiles decorate the ceiling vaults in Mercer's library, while the frieze above the fireplace opening is composed of "New World" brocade panels.

⁌ Opposite. One of Fonthill's numerous fireplaces presents a delightful mix of both flat mosaic tiles and brocade tiles in higher relief. The frieze extolls the "blessed toil" in evidence throughout Mercer's eccentric home.

The house was planned ... by me in the winter of 1907, room by room, entirely from the interior, the exterior not being considered until all the rooms had been imagined and sketched, after which blocks of clay representing the rooms were piled on a table, set together and modeled into a general outline. After a good many changes in the profile of tower, roofs, etc., a plaster-of-paris model was made to scale, and used until the building was completed.

The result of this modeling is one of the most romantic follies in America. The effect inside is all drama, heightened by Mercer's use of his own tile. As with the exterior, the surfaces of exposed concrete are part of the show. Colorful tiles are attached in places, enriching the already dramatic appearance of the rooms. On the floors are Mercer's "mosaic" tiles—flat pieces arranged to form designs. On the walls he used what he called "brocade" tiles modeled in high relief and set into the wet concrete, which serves as a background for the individual pieces. All of the forty-four rooms were handled in this manner.

Both inside and out, Fonthill contains allusions in form and detail to trips Mercer had taken and buildings he loved—departure points for his imagination, which roamed freely. Although Mercer used modern materials at Fonthill, everything is handcrafted in the Arts and Crafts manner and expresses his personal eclecticism.

❑ Left. The bed in this dormer bedroom nestles under an archway robed in tiles. Tucked into the soffits are Mercer's "Floral Brocade" tiles, brightening the reinforced-concrete walls.

❑ Below. In the Morning Room the chimneypiece is embroidered with Mercer's "Italian Brocade" tile pattern. The studded door adds one more decorative flourish.

63

CRAFTSMAN FARMS

Gustav Stickley (1857–1942) is an enigma. He counted himself a follower of William Morris, dedicating the first issue of his *Craftsman* magazine (1901–16) to the great English socialist and reformer. In it he wrote: "The United Crafts [Stickley's furniture factory] endeavor to promote and to extend the principles established by Morris, in both the artistic and the socialistic sense. In the interests of art, they seek to substitute the luxury of taste for the luxury of costliness."

Stickley's furniture, however, was very expensive by the standards of his day. The phrase "luxury of taste" suggests an even greater problem—an elitist view that Morris would not have liked. Of course, Stickley was no socialist. In *No Place of Grace* (Pantheon, 1981), the only scholarly study that tries to make sense of the Craftsman movement, Jackson Lears points to the fact that Stickley, along with other devotees, had a tendency to interpret Ruskin and Morris in a way that was almost the opposite of their intentions. Whereas the two Englishmen championed hand labor as a means of freeing workers from the monotony of machine production, Stickley and other American craftsmen did so as part of a discipline allowing spontaneity and freshness to thrive in a machine civilization. According to Lears, Stickley was concerned that American workers were becoming lazy as a result of mass production. As Stickley himself put it, the danger was "premature old age."

Only a few years after launching *The Craftsman*, Stickley addressed the evils of labor unions. He shared the fear of most political Progressives that organized labor was a threat to capitalism and agreed with Teddy Roosevelt's distinction between good and bad trusts—the bad should be prosecuted, the good left alone. In fact, he bought a tall office building in New York City and became, in essence, a capitalist himself.

Just as significant is the fact that he failed as a capitalist and that *The Craftsman* failed at about the same time. During its existence, the journal was one of the most interesting magazines in America. Barry Parker, who with Raymond Unwin was a leader in the British garden city movement, wrote thirty articles for it illustrating the duo's work. For a time *The Craftsman* was edited by Irene Sargent, a brilliant professor of romance languages at the University of Syracuse. More radical than Stickley, she published favorable reviews of Prince Kropotkin, a "genial" anarchist whom she liked more for his call for a return to cottage industry than for his revolutionary ideas. The tilemaker Ernest Batchelder's many essays in *The Craftsman* were collected to make his second book, *Design in Theory and Practice* (1910).

Gustav Stickley · 1910
Parsippany, New Jersey

64

❦ Stickley's house at Craftsman Farms is a typical bungalow of a story and a half, except that what in California would be a front porch has been filled in with windows. Building with notched chestnut logs put him in touch with both nature and America's pioneering roots.

❧ Above. Copper hooded fireplaces, each with an inscription, stake out the ends of Stickley's living room. This one is taken from Chaucer's *Parliament of Fowls*: "The lyf so short, the craft so long to lerne," a sentiment that graced the cover of Stickley's first issue of *The Craftsman* in 1901. As the other hood in the library nook proclaims, "By hammer and hand do all things stand."

❧ Left. The log walls and stone fireplace in the living room create a suitably rustic back-drop for examples of the furniture maker's work—rectilinear oak furniture softened by willow chairs, all from his own company. Stickley's S monogram is carved into the simple balusters framing the staircase.

The Craftsman became a kind of barometer of the American Arts and Crafts movement. The dwindling substance of its pages was pretty much the story of the movement, although the latter actually lasted well into the 1920s. Stickley was not so lucky. His financial woes led him to sell the Craftsman Building in New York City in 1917 and retreat with his family to his temporary sanctuary, Craftsman Farms, the small estate he had bought in New Jersey, about thirty miles from Manhattan. He called it his Eden.

The one-and-one-half-story house, built in 1910, is a California bungalow. At first glance, it is not particularly attractive on the exterior, but closer inspection shows that it is in a sense the ultimate Craftsman retreat into the wilderness—a log cabin. Stickley intended that the building serve as a school for students of the arts and crafts, but apart from a few changes, such as turning a part of the living room into a dining area, it remained as built. His hopes for a model farm and a community of craftsmen here also never materialized. The furniture was mainly United Crafts manufactures, expensive then and even more expensive today.

The Stickleys lived in the house for only a short time, selling it in 1918. In the late 1980s the house came on the market again, and for a time it seemed that what was left of the estate would be developed as a real estate project: the important modern architect Robert A. M. Stern was to design townhouses to harmonize with the old building, which would be used as a social center for the community. Since a preservation crusade, however, the Stickley house has been administered as a private museum.

Stickley was a rather poor designer—he was not an architect and instead hired professionals to design the Craftsman houses promoted in his publication—but Craftsman Farms is an important monument to a great force. With its pages of bungalows, cottages, and comfortable estates alongside inexpensive mail-order plans, Stickley's *Craftsman* served as the chief organ of the Arts and Crafts movement in America. And the man himself, in spite of his problems, has become an icon to Arts and Crafts adherents.

❰ Opposite. Stickley's spartan dining set and china cabinet almost disappear against the dining room's chinked log walls. Later owners painted the logs white throughout the house, but they have since been returned to their natural appearance.

❰ Below. To fit the long, narrow dining room, a long sideboard of oak and chestnut was custom made for one wall. A second dining set and sideboard also occupy the space, which the family made use of for parties.

68

❦ Above. As the book-lined walls of his living room testify, Stickley "read all the while," according to his daughter Mildred. His 1902 Eastwood chair—sturdy, capacious, and perfectly upright—named for his first factory in Eastwood, New York, offered the perfect spot to read away the evening.

❦ Left. Furniture in the daughters' bedroom is entirely from Stickley's United Crafts, while the blue tiles surrounding the fireplace came from Grueby, a popular Arts and Crafts tilemaker. The rug here reverses the colorway seen on the examples in the living area. Similar geometric patterns were used for the wool rugs Stickley made for customers.

SIMPLE LIVING, HIGH THINKING

FREEMAN HOUSE

In addition to the British Arts and Crafts movement, the American Craftsman aesthetic had yet another source: H. H. Richardson (1838–86), a southerner who went to Harvard and, like other designers featured in this book, was transformed by it. He did not exactly become a Yankee, but in his life and work he developed styles in both public and domestic architecture intended to be emblematic of America's cultural rise. His architecture was both stylish and sound.

Richardson was one of the American architects who adapted the Queen Anne style of Richard Norman Shaw (1831–1912) to create Shingle Style houses. His Watts Sherman House (1874) in Newport, Rhode Island, is usually regarded as the style's first monument. From it—the shingles on the outside and the wood panels inside—would evolve the woodsy Craftsman style of house. But Richardson's public architecture—churches, libraries, schools, and commercial buildings—also lay behind the work of Louis Sullivan, Frank Lloyd Wright, and other architects identified with the American Arts and Crafts movement.

Ernest Coxhead · 1903
Berkeley, California

❦ Left. An otherwise Georgian facade is broken up by Dutch gambrel-roofed gables and is extended by a wing that seems added on but was part of the original building. The dappled roof, in contrast, probably replaced a shingled roof after the Berkeley fire of 1923.

❦ Below. Framed in an archway of the porch is a lantern that lends a quaint Asian touch to an otherwise English vernacular house. Coxhead's commingling of styles was his signature.

Perhaps even more important was Richardson's influence on the smaller names of American architecture in the late nineteenth and early twentieth centuries. These were the people who designed in his style and whose Richardsonian Romanesque buildings can be found in almost every city and small town in the country. One spectacular example in the West is the First Congregational Church (1889) in Colorado Springs, Colorado, pictured on page 24. Richardsonian outside, it is pure Craftsman inside.

Ernest Coxhead (1863–1933) fits nicely into this kind of eclecticism. In several of his own seventeen built churches he employs a similar witch's-hat motif for the roof, but more important is the fact that he was a Richardsonian who, even though an Englishman by birth, was attracted to the architecture of the most important American architect of his day. Coxhead, born in the seaside resort of Eastbourne in Sussex, was articled (apprenticed) to an engineer involved in creating public amenities for the resort. Working on residential projects as well, the young Coxhead decided to become an architect. Gothic architecture inspired him to make drawings of medieval churches.

On taking a job as a draftsman with a London architect, he entered the Royal Academy of Fine Arts. There he had the unusual experience (for a British student) of being introduced by a teacher, Richard Phené Spiers, to the method of the Ecole des Beaux-Arts in Paris. Spiers was able to give Coxhead a sense of classical order, in contrast to the Gothic order with which he was already familiar. Coxhead's Beaux-Arts training would make him conscious of what he was doing when he broke with it in his American practice. Significantly, just before he moved to the United States he became interested in the English vernacular architecture that was such an influence on Britain's Arts and Crafts architects.

Probably his move to California had something to do with Coxhead's ability as a church architect. After opening an office in Los Angeles in 1887, at the height of a land boom, he was employed to design a series of Episcopal churches up and down California from Red Bluff to Santa Ana. Often dollhouse in scale, these were typically Richardsonian Romanesque with a few Gothic intrusions.

By 1890, his church-designing days about over, he moved to the Bay Area and focused on domestic architecture, simplifying the English vernacular and shingling it. The Freeman House, known as Allenoke Manor, is a prime example of his allegiance to the vernacular tradition of C.F.A. Voysey and other English architects. But unlike Voysey, Coxhead emphasized rusticity much more strongly than did the English Arts and Crafts architects.

❦ Right. The Freeman House, like all of Ernest Coxhead's residential interiors, contains great surprises. In the living room the understated fireplace is almost Georgian in its serenity. Yet off to the right, a grand staircase strikes a pleasantly contrasting note. Drawing all together, a heavily beamed ceiling brings the room down to human scale.

Here at Allenoke Manor he uses brick, but it is clinker brick—never so gnarled as the overfired brick that Charles and Henry Greene used—and irregular enough to have a mottled effect that clashes with the house's classical elements. The front facade, with its two huge gambrel dormers to the left, is obviously intended to contradict the proportions and forms of the other side, which looks as if it had been added on. A broad Richardsonian arch over the porch is out of proportion to the dormers and variegated details but thereby adds a consciously picturesque touch to the house, as if Coxhead were parodying the English vernacular. The interior spaces of his houses offer the same picturesque surprises as do their exterior and interior details.

Coxhead never really bared his soul over the buildings he created, so it is tempting to see this studied awkwardness as a reflection of North Berkeley's topography, which in its hills and dales invites irregularities. Charles Keeler, a spokesman for Bernard Maybeck's romantic Berkeley houses, wrote in *The Simple Home* (1904) that the beauty of a town such as Berkeley, set on rolling hills, is that its streets, undulating along the contours of these hills, will make for irregular lot dimensions "so that unconventional groups of buildings may be set upon the landscape in the most picturesque fashion."

❮ Left. Coxhead's fireplace in the Freeman dining room would seem almost modern if relieved of the swords placed above the firebox. Other fireplaces of his, such as at the Earl House (1895–98) in Los Angeles, were incredible baroque extravaganzas.

❮ Opposite. The staircase in the Freeman House is reminiscent of the rich profusion of a Stanford White stairway. A landing reached by just a few steps creates the effect of a screen. The balustrade is long and low, and its closely spaced balusters provide a dramatic background that contrasts with the simplicity of the living room fireplace.

HEWITT HOUSE

How could an architect be a sophisticated classicist and at the same time champion Craftsman rusticity? Edwin Hawley Hewitt (1874–1939) is not usually associated with the Craftsman movement. His buildings in Minneapolis and surrounding areas were typically churches and office buildings in variations of Beaux-Arts styles. But when he designed his own house, he chose the Tudor version of Craftsman architecture with a little Prairie style thrown in. Perhaps more understandably, Hewitt in 1913 produced another Craftsman house, decorated outside with Arts and Crafts tiles, for the founder of the Handicraft Guild of Minneapolis.

Born in Red Wing, Minnesota, Hewitt was graduated from the University of Minnesota in 1895. During summer vacations he worked in the office of Cass Gilbert (1859–1934), whose first major commission was the Minnesota State Capitol (1893–1904) but whose

Edwin Hawley Hewitt · 1906
Minneapolis

most famous building was the Woolworth Tower (1913) in New York City. After an additional year of study, at the Massachusetts Institute of Technology, Hewitt joined the office of another famous architecture firm, Shepley, Rutan and Coolidge, which had inherited the practice of H. H. Richardson (1838–86). Hewitt's architectural training was crowned by his study at the Ecole des Beaux-Arts in Paris, where he took a degree in 1904, ranking second in a class of fifty. Thus he was well trained in the neoclassical tradition that admired order and attention to function. Accepting the Ecole's philosophy of eclecticism—after developing a rational plan, the architect should cover it with plenty of ornament drawn from all of the historic styles—Hewitt used Gothic, Renaissance, and baroque forms on his public buildings.

81

❧ Left. A duo of prominent stucco front gables framing a central section links Edwin Hawley Hewitt's house to English Arts and Crafts architecture. A balcony covers the entrance.

❧ Below. In contrast to the upper two stories, the ground floor shows the horizontality that was a hallmark of the American Prairie style. Most likely the source was Frank Lloyd Wright's projecting and receding brickwork on the Heurtley House (1902) in Oak Park, Illinois.

Opposite. The fireplace near the front door mixes tiles from Henry Mercer's Moravian Pottery and Tile Works with a copper hood created by the Handicraft Guild of Minneapolis. Most of the tiles are from common stock, but a few show a primitive picture-writing motif that may have been inspired by Mayan glyphs.

Below left. For the hearth Hewitt chose Henry Mercer's "mosaic" tiles depicting an Indian lighting a fire. Hexagonal pacer tiles found here are repeated on the floors of the hall, living room, and sunroom.

Below right. Decorative tile marking the opening of the living room fireplace is Mercer's "Knight of Morgam," inspired by a similar tile the Pennsylvania tilemaker saw displayed on the floor of Morgam Abbey.

The architect's own house, designed before he joined Edwin Hacker Brown in a partnership that lasted from 1911 to 1930, has an unusual facade. Its second and third stories, apart from the heavy fenestration, are closely related in style to the English vernacular, which was fundamental to the work of the British Arts and Crafts architects. But the treatment of the ground-floor exterior, with its striations of brick in two shades of red, departs from the English vernacular even more than the window treatment.

For the coppery-toned interior Hewitt collaborated with Mary Linton Bookwalter, an interior designer well versed in the Craftsman aesthetic. As Patty Dean has noted in *Minnesota History,* in this house Bookwalter achieved "continuity through textiles," using a "green-and-tan canvas resembling dullish copper" on the beamed ceilings of the hall, living room, and dining room; "a rug of 'squared animals' and alphabet letters and matching curtains in an indigo-blue and tan palette" for the Hewitts' three-year-old daughter's room; and "a piece of Japanese embroidery in gray-green, tan and soft rose on a cloudy gray ground, [which] inspired the colors and decorative glass motifs of the sunroom."

Almost all of this decoration is now gone, as is the furniture, an eclectic mix. Hewitt was much more interested in curiosities than in designing furniture to match the house. Strongly influenced by his Minneapolis friend John S. Bradstreet, an orientalist, he strewed Japanese artifacts—shoji screens, lamps and lanterns, and, of course, textiles—everywhere. The third floor housed his collection of Japanese sword handles.

Hewitt's intention to make his house an embodiment of Craftsman principles is clear in his choice of materials for the fireplace in the front hall. Like many midwestern architects, including Frank Lloyd Wright, he used Mercer tiles, in this case in the surround, some of them molded into patterns reflecting primitive picture writing. Over the firebox he placed a copper hood fabricated at the studios of the Handicraft Guild of Minneapolis; its ornament of facing birds was probably inspired by Mercer designs and carried out by Douglas Donaldson, who also worked with Ernest Batchelder (1875–1957) of Pasadena at the guild.

83

In 1907 Gustav Stickley's *Craftsman* carried an article on Hewitt's house entitled "A House of Harmonies: The Effect of a Happy Combination of Personal Interest and Professional Skill." It is filled with a didacticism that is probably Bookwalter's:

The house shall be so planned, decorated and furnished that each separate detail shall be apparent only as an unobtrusive part of one well-balanced whole.... The decorator has to steer a very careful course between the restlessness of too great contrast in strongly individual features and the equal restlessness produced by a sense of monotony in color and form.... The most satisfying results are gained only when there is a keen personal interest in the work; nothing done by professional architect or decorator ... can have the little intimate touch of individuality that arises only from expression of personal taste and direct response to the needs of the life that is to be lived in the house.

This credo comes about as close as possible to a definition of the interior designer's relation to the Craftsman aesthetic—devotion to the lifestyle of the occupant of the house. But why a Craftsman house for Hewitt? The same question could be asked of other classically trained architects of the day, among them Bernard Maybeck and Julia Morgan, who chose the woodsy Craftsman aesthetic for various houses. One easy answer is that the Craftsman style symbolized for them as for so many others simple living leading to high thinking.

❧ Above. A sunroom window design was taken from Japanese embroidery used for the portière that hung in the doorway between the sunroom and the living room.

❧ Opposite. Struts under the gables' high eaves terminate in carved dragonheads, modeled on details from Japanese temples.

BAILEY HOUSE

"**W**e should build our house simple, plain and substantial as a boulder, then leave the ornamentation to Nature, who will tone it with lichens, chisel it with storms, make it gracious and friendly with vines and flower shadows as she does the stone in the meadow." This declaration by Irving Gill (1870–1936), which appeared in the May 1916 issue of *The Craftsman*, combines two divergent strains of architectural thought. One, the rationalist approach, suggests a process of elimination that would divest a building of ornament or any other reference to historic styles. The second strain is romantic: ornament is acceptable but only if applied by nature through a process of aging and reflection of natural forms and colors. Gill's own architectural pilgrimage led from the romantic to the rationalist.

Irving Gill, with Frank Mead
1907 · La Jolla, California

He grew up in Syracuse, New York, where he worked in an architect's office for a short time. After hearing about Louis Sullivan (1856–1924), the great Chicago architect, Gill determined to go west and work for him. His dream was realized in 1890, when Sullivan hired him as a draftsman. It is dangerous to speculate on Sullivan's influence on the young man. The two years that Gill spent in the Adler and Sullivan office were during the height of the firm's activity, and the two likely had little opportunity to say much to each other. Surely Sullivan's "Form follows function" dictum must have been discussed in the office, but probably with other young apprentices rather than with the master, as Frank Lloyd Wright, another Sullivan employee, referred to him. Perhaps Gill was familiar with Sullivan's remark that it might be better for architects to give up ornament for a time to get back to the fundamentals of architecture—a suggestion that Sullivan himself found impossible to follow. But it was a heady remedy at a time when Victorian and Beaux-Arts excess was being challenged.

86

❦ Below and right. As several critics have pointed out, Irving Gill came very close to the modern movement taking place at the same time in Europe. His paring away to the geometry of architecture in the Bailey House mirrors modernist ideas, except that here his arrangement of volumes and fenestration is awkward. The view, however, is marvelous.

❆ Above. Wheeler Bailey asked Gill to take his inspiration for the house from barns. He probably meant the interior features, but here the sliding front doors resemble rather elegant barn doors.

❆ Right. Gill would be delighted with the way nature has decorated this house. His pergola was a strong invitation.

❦ Above. In contrast to the exterior's cool stucco walls, natural redwood used inside for the board-and-batten walls and the ceiling lend the Bailey House the air of a friendly barn. Bailey furnished his house with furniture from Stickley and Gill and had a large assemblage of American Indian arts.

❦ Left. In the living room two elevated hayloft doors allow views down from the second-story bedrooms. They help create a high overmantel for the rustic stone hearth.

In 1892, suffering from bad health, Gill moved to California, the ultimate recuperative center. In San Diego he found not only a healthful climate but also a young city (population 17,000) that needed architects. At first he worked on his own, then with Joseph Falkenham, and then with an older architect, William S. Hebbard (1863–1930); during the latter period he produced his exceptional Los Baños (1897), a local bathhouse that merged details from California missions and Islamic architecture. Gill's designs, although in eclectic styles, showed a desire for simplification that would become his chief interest.

In the Mission Revival style Gill found a framework for simplification, because behind its Moorish towers, *campanario*-derived gables, and oriel windows was a suggestion of abstraction. Elimination of these decorative details resulted in the pure architecture that Sullivan desired but could not achieve. From this point on Gill would, with occasional lapses into the past, pare away the details to architecture's essentials.

The Bailey House represents the turning point in Gill's architecture from romantic to rationalist. The exterior, especially the side facing the ocean, is a simplification of the Mission Revival style. The facade is almost pure geometry; the only traces of a mission are the rounded arches. The woodsy Craftsman interior, however, is another matter. Wheeler Bailey seems to have asked Gill to design an interior that looked like a barn, and Gill seems to have acquiesced: he left the redwood board-and-batten walls natural with no stain or varnish, equipped the entrance with sliding barn doors, and designed a pair of hayloft doors that open onto the living room from the second story.

Charles Lummis visited the house on July 28, 1915, just after touring the Panama-California Exposition in San Diego, where he had seen his friend Teddy Roosevelt. Bailey was a "funny old bachelor ... who has built an uncommonly cozy nest right out on the edge of the cliffs at La Jolla and has gathered a good many Indian relics of the buyable sort," Lummis noted in his memoirs. Down the street was Bailey's Hopi house, commissioned from the San Diego firm of Mead and Requa. A specialist on the Indians of the Southwest, Lummis commented, "I suppose it would make a Hopi laugh to see his desert architecture up there—since the only ocean he ever saw is the sea of endless sands, without enough water to irrigate a blade of grass."

After 1907 Gill focused on simplification. He experimented with concrete, itself a kind of discipline that dictated economy of decorative effect. Another factor in Gill's experiments in eliminating unnecessary details may have been his short partnership with Frank Mead (1865–1940), who had traveled widely in North Africa and had admired the native architecture there. Whatever the influences, including Sullivan's strictures, Gill used wood ever more sparingly and, when he did, avoided the rustic quality of the Bailey House interiors. But in the Bailey House, as in his earlier work, he was a stylist, an eclectic, following in the line of other Craftsman designers, manipulating nature but never losing the human touch.

93

❦ No Craftsman house would be complete without a built-in sideboard in the dining room. The prominent hinges on these cupboard doors show that Gill was acquainted with the work of English Arts and Crafts designers, especially M. H. Baillie Scott.

EVANS HOUSE

After the disastrous San Francisco earthquake and fire of 1906, the phoenix often rose elsewhere. Many San Franciscans, concerned about proximity to the San Andreas Fault, decided to rebuild in nearby Marin County, above the area where the fault turned out into the ocean. Ernest and Letitia Evans were among these émigrés. They had chosen Bernard Maybeck (1862–1957) as their architect but, finding him too radical, hired the newly arrived Louis Christian Mullgardt. Mullgardt (1866–1942) was born in Washington, Missouri, to German immigrant parents. Although he early showed talent as a painter, printmaker, and sculptor, his real love was architecture. His training was as an apprentice in architecture offices in St. Louis, Boston, and Chicago.

Louis Christian Mullgardt
1907 · Mill Valley, California

Like Horace Greeley's young man, Mullgardt went west to San Francisco in 1905, where he was employed by the prestigious firm of Willis Polk (1867–24). The firm split up in the year of the fire, so he was on his own when the Evanses recognized his ability and commissioned him to design their house for a picturesque hillside in Mill Valley, in the shadow of Mount Tamalpais.

Marin County is one of the most beautiful areas in a very beautiful state, attractive to San Franciscans even before the earthquake. Many people liked to hike in nature's wonderland or stay a night or two at one of the resort hotels that were beginning to dot the place. As transportation facilities made it less remote, its value as a suburb of San Francisco was recognized. Yet the idea of remaining rural continued to be held sacred.

94

❦ Right. The high-waisted appearance of the Evans House—with wood siding changing to stucco at the second-story sill line—recalls Frank Lloyd Wright's division of his Prairie houses to stress their horizontality. An entrance pergola tying the house to nature was never built.

❦ Below. Daringly cantilevered over its steep lot in Mill Valley, outside San Francisco, the house brings to mind quaint Swiss chalets yet has overtones of a Japanese temple.

❰ Above. Board-and-batten walls in the entrance hall reverse the horizontal geometry of the exterior. The architect's plan to create a perfect ensemble by designing all the furniture for the Evans House proved too expensive, although some light fixtures are still in place.

❰ Right. In line with the emerging organic theory of architecture, the staircase balusters reflect the pattern of the windows. Storage is neatly tucked into the redwood paneling below to make use of every space. The house remains in almost its original condition.

❰ Opposite, far right. The interior is laid out so that most rooms open out to a patio or to this porch, allowing for indoor-outdoor living in tune with nature. The Golden Gate is another incentive to take in the spectacular view.

Opposite. At the heart of the Evans House's simple rectangular plan is a brick fireplace ornamented with quoins and a copper hood. The rectilinear stair balusters make an appropriate backdrop for the current owners' furniture, which is principally Stickley or Stickleyesque.

Below. Board-and-batten redwood paneling used throughout the downstairs, as Robert Judson Clark has noticed, still gives off its mellowed fragrance of the forest. Friezes running above offer a respite from the wood.

According to the *San Francisco Call* in 1889, the year that Mill Valley was platted, residents desired "a place nearby where they can get close to nature—not an artificial park, but nature unadorned." A civil engineer, Michael O'Shaughnessy, was hired to lay out a plan. Following an idea that had already been used in Berkeley, he designed the streets to follow the contours of the undulating land. As Richard Longstreth has observed in *On the Edge of the World* (1983), O'Shaughnessy broke with the conventional American gridiron plan—the system imposed on San Francisco's hills, ironically making the city so picturesque—and designed streets sympathetic to Mill Valley's natural terrain, much like Frederick Law Olmsted's 1869 plan for Riverside, Illinois.

For this picturesque setting Mullgardt decided to base his ideas for the Evans House, also known as Tamaledge, on the Swiss chalet mode. A rectangle in plan, it was organized around a central fireplace and was cantilevered into the view with a partly open rear porch high in the treetops. Herbert Croly, editor of *Architectural Record*, wrote an article on Mullgardt in 1911, in which he alluded strongly to the architect's affinity for the site:

The best of Mullgardt's houses are molded to their sites; they are softened and enveloped by the neighboring foliage; they are warmed and tinted by the sunlight; and they give one the sense of breathing the very air. In short, they have a way of appearing to live on the spot where they happen to have been put. . . . Mark the way in which the skyline of the house continues and completes the skyline of the hill, and the way the salient chimney rises at just the right point for the purpose of tying together the two slopes of the hill. . . . Back of it all is a gift that enabled the architect . . . to design a house for which the hill had been waiting since the day of its birth.

99

Mullgardt's attitude toward nature is also evidenced by his concern for the approach to the house. He designed a long pergola leading to the front door. Unfortunately, it was never built, but his intention to lead the visitor to the house through vines shows his desire to build with nature.

The house's relation to nature is underscored in the dining room as well as in the living room by a wide swath of French doors on the south side, leading out to the porch. As in most Craftsman houses, the windows are casement—all the better to reach out to nature. Here they showcase art glass resembling a shoji screen. Letitia Evans had been a missionary in China and loved Asian art; both she and Ernest vacationed in Japan whenever they could.

After playing with Swiss and Japanese allusions in the Evans House, Mullgardt went on to probe other Asian sources. When a critic suggested that his layered Taylor House (1908) in Berkeley resembled the Potala at Lhassa, he answered that, yes, the Tibetans had been copying him for centuries. For his wildly popular Court of the Ages at the Panama-Pacific Exposition of 1915 in San Francisco, he chose what has been called the "Portuguese Gothic" style. Obviously his Arts and Crafts days had come to an end.

CALDWELL HOUSE

The Arts and Crafts movement, always limited to a relatively small group, rarely affected mass culture. The one exception occurred in public and private schools, where manual training was introduced in the late nineteenth century as part of a curriculum that also emphasized the humanities and sciences. At that time the National Education Association encouraged technical education in addition to the standard course of study, and shop work and domestic science remained requirements even in college preparatory curriculums well into the 1930s.

If William Morris, who never liked Americans very much anyway, could have seen what was really going on, however, he would not have been pleased. Although many schools prided themselves on stressing the cooperation of head and heart with hand, the effect of introducing manual training was eventually to separate the doers from the thinkers. The Craftsman period of 1895–1920 was an age in which specialization was advancing in every field, including education. Lip service might be given to the idea of the well-rounded person, but history was on the side of the well-trained expert. The crafts worker became irrelevant, relegated to technical high schools and eventually to blue-collar occupations.

Louis B. Easton · 1907
Sierra Madre, California

It was during this period, in 1890, that Louis B. Easton (1864–1921) received his teaching credentials in manual training from the Bloomington (Illinois) Normal School. There he had fallen in love with Honor Hubbard, the youngest sister of Elbert Hubbard, who was pursuing the same degree. Their romance blossomed into marriage. Easton got a job teaching manual training at Lemont High School, south of Chicago, and in 1893 became the school's principal. While teaching, he was also designing and making furniture much along the lines of the foursquare work of Gustav Stickley, whose *Craftsman* magazine he surely became familiar with. In 1903 some of Easton's work was shown in an Arts and Crafts exhibition at the Art Institute of Chicago.

101

❡ Left. A street-facing gable sporting wooden crosspieces is an Easton trademark. "The broad, overhanging eaves of the roof," noted *The Craftsman* in March 1908, "add much to the effect of coolness, which is further emphasized by the deeply recessed porch."

❡ Right. Hardware on the front door shows its age. The wood grain was purposely brought out with a wire brush.

At about this time Easton discovered that he had respiratory problems requiring a healthier climate. California beckoned. He settled in Pasadena, and almost immediately his health improved. Drawing on his ability as a carpenter, he decided to build a house for his growing family. Although he had no training in architectural design, he found a book illustrating bungalows, used it as a guide, and produced a fairly decent-looking house. Gaining confidence, he built another house, this time trusting his own judgment rather than the book.

Both houses have all the trappings of a typical Craftsman house: brown stained exteriors and interiors with simple brick fireplaces, redwood paneling, beamed ceilings, copper hardware, and built-in fixtures. They were much admired and established Easton as a clever designer. A career in architecture and furniture making followed.

The Caldwell House in Sierra Madre is one of Easton's legacy of about twenty-five houses of simple beauty. By the time he received the commission, another architect had drawn a floor plan and the foundation had been built, so Easton had to design within this framework. The house had been sited so that southern light would brighten the front rooms. Easton eliminated almost all the interior partitions so that except for the kitchen wing, the interior was only one room deep. This arrangement not only brought in light but also allowed fresh air to flow through the rooms whichever way the wind was blowing—an important asset in a town that had several tuberculosis sanitariums and whose citizens were extremely concerned about proper ventilation.

The house's exterior is somewhat unusual. The gable facing the street has wooden crosspieces that serve as a kind of ornament, for they have no real function. The two wings, sited at almost forty-five-degree angles to the main house, are similarly covered with redwood siding. Elsewhere cedar shingles appear. Native fieldstone foundations, parapets, and columns add to the rustic effect.

The March 1908 issue of *The Craftsman* rhapsodized about the Caldwell House:

The house gives the impression of being well connected with the ground upon which it stands. The redwood siding and trim and the cedar shingles are simply oiled and left to weather, the rich reddish-brown tone of the redwood blending with the silvery brownish-gray of the cedar and the varying colors in the stone, into a general effect of warm grayish-brown which is in perfect harmony with the dull tawny colors that predominate in the landscape during the greater part of the year.

The writer closed with this assessment: "The house is an admirable illustration of the adaptation of a dwelling to the climate and surroundings, and the preservation of harmony between the exterior and interior of the house.... It is distinctively Californian, but full of suggestion for the building of any country house or summer residence."

With the coming of World War I, home construction declined. Easton concluded his adventure in architecture and moved to Anaheim, where he engaged in truck farming until his death. Technology had ended Easton's career only indirectly, but his change in vocation echoed the loss of dynamism in the Craftsman movement. Modernization was in the saddle.

❪ Above. The dining room staircase has been restored. "Placed as it is," commented *The Craftsman,* "the stairway is convenient for the use of the family and is also near enough to the door used by the servants without disturbing the rest of the household."

❪ Opposite. The Caldwell House's simple but elegant sideboard is built in to conserve space. Like the front door, its wood is also brushed to make the grain stand out.

GLESS AND HINDRY HOUSES

A great many people in Pasadena who live in bungalows like to think that their homes were designed by Charles and Henry Greene. Most bungalows in fact were not even influenced by the Greenes, although some are very good Craftsman designs in their own right. A pair of designers responsible for numerous handsome bungalows, and whose work most closely resembles the Greenes', are Arthur S. Heineman (1878–1972) and his brother, Alfred (1882–1974). During their partnership lasting until around 1939, they designed many houses in Pasadena and the West Adams neighborhood of Los Angeles, including the bungalows lining Pasadena's Bowen Court (1910) (see page 27).

Arthur S. Heineman, with
Alfred Heineman, associate
1910–11 and 1908–9
Los Angeles and Pasadena,
California

The brothers, who had come to Los Angeles in 1894 and later began to deal in real estate, soon realized that land sold more quickly with a house on it. Although neither had any training in architecture, Arthur—a bit of an inventor who was good with clients—learned to sketch floor plans, while the artistic Alfred took charge of the drawings; he later claimed that he took only one formal design course, from the tilemaker and design theorist Ernest Batchelder (1875–1957) at the old Throop Polytechnic Institute, now the California Institute of Technology.

❡ Opposite. A fireplace in the front hall of the Gless House in Los Angeles is crowned with a cantilevered staircase landing. Its perforated balustrade acts as a screen for the soaring space above, which was a trademark of the Heineman brothers.

❡ Below. Featuring a wide porch and an art glass entrance, the front of the Gless House exhibits a mixture of Tudor and Bavarian styles. Two second-story porches, one for sleeping and the other for enjoying the California air, face a rear garden.

❰ Above. From the walls and built-in cabinets to the ceiling, the dining room of the Gless House is cloaked in a woodsy Craftsman frame. A plate rail picks up the space's dominant horizontality.

❰ Opposite and right. Over the curved built-in sideboard in the Gless dining room, art glass windows illustrate the Old King Cole rhyme. Alfred Heineman noted that he always designed his own glass, which was fabricated by "that funny little company in Garvanza"—the renowned Judson Studios, which was actually located in downtown Los Angeles until 1921.

After he joined Arthur's real estate firm about 1909—he had already designed several bungalows with another brother, Herbert—Alfred continued designing small houses and succeeded in selling his ideas to Edward E. Sweet's design and building company. One of its brochures featured a Heineman bungalow in color on the cover and also illustrated Alfred's designs inside. According to Alfred, so many Heineman buildings started going up that well-trained local architects encouraged Arthur to become a registered architect so that it did not appear that amateurs could replace them. He did what he could to prepare for the examination and passed.

The Heinemans' approach—coupling architecture with real estate sales—proved extremely successful. As their practice grew, the brothers attracted clients who could afford larger houses. Exploring the Japanese-Swiss idiom so closely associated with California, these commissions recalled what the Greenes were designing but were much less expensive. Where the Greenes used teak, the Heinemans used gum woods. And whereas the Greenes almost always expected to design the furniture for their houses, the Heinemans made no such demands, allowing their clients to express their own taste and use hand-me-downs.

The Heinemans' work never quite matched the quality of the Greenes,' but they sensed—perhaps by accident—that architecture was something more than fine building. Their interest lay in the manipulation of space, an intuition foreign to the Greenes, whose floor plans were conventional. In contrast, the Heinemans loved to use diagonals in their plans. Their entrances might be straightforward, but almost immediately after crossing the threshold the visitor is led to change direction with a confusion—and delight—that would please Robert Venturi's notions of complexity and contradiction in architecture. Similarly, in designing stair halls they used vertical space to make viewers look up as well as from side to side. Neither was a Frank Lloyd Wright, but they understood the drama of space.

❦ The vertiginous entrance hall of the Hindry House in Pasadena shows the Heinemans' mastery of space. Just inside the door awaits a surprise: a huge boulder fireplace. To its right is the dining room, which at its far end is separated from a breakfast room by a screen of clear beveled glass in geometric patterns.

◖ Above left. A Craftsman clock has been fitted into the boulder fireplace in the Hindry entry—a bit of Heineman whimsy. To the left of the fireplace, which Charles Greene may have designed, rises a subdued staircase beneath a flattened Tudor arch.

◖ Above right. A quieter yet still impressive brick fireplace with a hammered-copper hood helps fill one wall of the living room. Built-in bookcases and molding continue its line for a seamless appearance. The chandeliers were designed by Alfred Heineman.

Like many architects of the period, the Heinemans found a variety of styles that allowed them variety in expression; they would not be limited by dogmatic consistency. The Hindry House (1908–9) in Pasadena and the Gless House (1910–11) in the Hancock Park district of Los Angeles are cases in point. The former is in the Mission Revival style, a relative of A. Page Brown's California State Building at the 1893 World's Columbian Exposition in Chicago, while the latter is an amalgam of English Tudor and Bavarian hunting lodge on the exterior. The Gless House is bigger and cost more, but both houses exhibit the Heinemans' joy in the manipulation of space.

The Gless House looks as if it has always stood at the corner of Sixth Street and Plymouth, but it was moved there from a site on Wilshire Boulevard in 1924. Anyone who feels empathy for structural logic will be utterly confused by the house. Its front hall is parallel neither to the street nor to the back wall behind the stair. A summer beam projects from near the front door but does not quite reach the staircase, where it might have found a footing. The stair landing seems to hang from two posts barely big enough to hold the weight. Steel may have been used in the house, but no bolts give away the structural skeleton. Was this construction an example of amateurish playfulness? Probably not. The engineering was provided by the Milwaukee Building Company, and the landing's floor does not creak when walked on even after a number of earthquakes have tested its strength. After these pyrotechnics, the other rooms in the house seem tame. Most are what Wright would call boxes, although elegant ones.

In the 1920s the Heinemans adopted the popular period revivals, while in the 1930s they got into Cape Coddage and Streamline Moderne. Shortly before his death, when Alfred was asked how he could have taken the Craftsman aesthetic so lightly, his reply was characteristically modest: "I guess we didn't know any better."

ROOS HOUSE

If there is a single key to the complex life of Bernard Maybeck (1862–1957), it is his love of drama. He dressed as a Pre-Raphaelite king in a red velvet robe and beret of his own design. He created costumes for the pageants his family loved and designed stage sets for amateur theatricals at the Hillside Club in Berkeley. His propensity for drama permeated his architecture too—his Palace of Fine Arts (1915) for the Panama-Pacific Exposition in San Francisco needed only Cecil B. De Mille and his extras to give it life. It is all drama, its flourish of classical details and huge planting boxes with inwardly facing figures capturing a spirit, as Maybeck said, of "sadness modified by the feeling that beauty has a soothing influence."

Maybeck was born into an active cultural life. His parents were European immigrants—his father a furniture maker and master builder, his mother from a family of intellectuals and political reformers. Maybeck's early education was fairly conventional, except that his inability to make himself memorize enough material to pass a compulsory chemistry course apparently forced his withdrawal from the College of the City of New York. A turn as an apprentice to a firm that designed furniture and architectural carving seemed more promising, but again Maybeck was bored with routine and did what many imaginative young men of that day did—he went to Paris, the traditional retreat of the young and the free.

Almost immediately Maybeck was attracted to the Ecole des Beaux-Arts; its unusually strict curriculum and organization might have seemed an odd choice for a somewhat rebellious young man. Yet even in his wildest buildings, Maybeck never forgot the school's lesson that a rational, functional floor plan was the basis for all architecture—albeit embellished with suitable ornament.

Bernard Maybeck · 1909
San Francisco

111

❮ Left and below. Two views of the Roos House exterior give an idea of Bernard Maybeck's incredible imagination. He begins with an unorthodox interpretation of Tudor black-and-white work, and then he adds quatrefoils to give the design a bit more spice. Planter boxes bring the architecture down to earth with a domestic touch to please any English gardener.

◖ Opposite. Maybeck wrenched every decorative possibility from the Roos House design, using a forest of braces to project the house into its hilly surroundings.

◖ Below. The south side of the Roos House, framed by a spacious veranda, perfectly captures Maybeck's eclecticism. Sober Tudoresque walls erupt into an elaborate covered balcony carrying a quatrefoil pattern—conjuring up the face of a Cheshire cat.

The same spirit of dramatic poetry Maybeck built into the Palace of Fine Arts infuses the house he designed for Elizabeth and Leon Roos in San Francisco. It was a wedding present from Elizabeth's father, Morris Meyerfeld, a partner in the Orpheum Theater Circuit Company. Many years earlier, accompanying her father on a talent search to Europe, Elizabeth had become infatuated with all things theatrical. When she learned that Maybeck designed theatrical houses, she chose him over another architect that her father had already picked out. She certainly got what she wanted.

Some might argue that the Roos House is too eclectic to be Craftsman. True, Maybeck's Mathewson House (1915) and Schneider-Kroeber House (1907) are on the exterior more like the simplified Swiss-Japanese image of many Arts and Crafts residences. But the Craftsman movement was eclectic, as the Japanese and Swiss connections attest. In the Roos House, Maybeck took eclectism about as far as it could go without becoming bizarre.

The exterior is Tudoresque with exaggerated Gothic details similar to those Maybeck used on the interior of the First Church of Christ, Scientist (1910) in Berkeley. A corridor along the east side of the house leads to the front door, decorated with a crest that Leon Roos himself designed for it. From the entrance hall Maybeck's adherence to one primary Beaux-Arts principle of design is visible: the house's north-south axis, which extends from the dining room through the living room. The view from the Rooses' living room is the ultimate in the picturesque, capturing the Presidio and San Francisco Bay while barely missing the Golden Gate Bridge.

The redwood-paneled dining room is lovely, but the living room, a baronial hall originally hung with silk banners, is where Maybeck's imagination was freed. The fireplace, modeled in cast plaster and concrete to look like stone, is a strange interpretation of the Tudor style. Electric lights dangle from the ceiling in clusters that Maybeck called "atmospheric lights," while higher up are starlike chandeliers. The room evokes the Middle Ages although no one in that period ever saw anything like it.

To help minimize the effects of earthquakes—the 1906 San Francisco temblor was fresh in everyone's mind—Maybeck devised an unusual foundation for the house, something like a raft floating on piles drilled into the earth. The garden that he planned no longer exists. Maybeck lived a very long life and designed many more houses. But the Roos House, his most elaborate, is one of his masterpieces.

❦ Opposite. Maybeck was known to dine with his clients to learn more about them. He gave the Rooses a dining room that is not large compared to the living room, but with its board-and-batten redwood paneling it is more like what we think of as Craftsman. The fireplace is vaguely Tudor although no one living in the sixteenth century would recognize it as such. The sconces seem to have been inspired by the helmets of medieval knights.

❦ Below left and right. The living room is furnished mainly with antiques that the Rooses collected on their trips to Europe, but Maybeck designed a couch and two chairs—decorated with quatrefoil molding, fleur-de-lis, and the Roos crest—to group around the stonelike fireplace. Chandeliers and hanging lights draw the eye up to the full height of the fireplace.

THOMAS HOUSE

Julia Morgan · 1911
Berkeley, California

Julia Morgan is best known as the architect of the Hearst Castle (1919–39) at San Simeon on California's central coast. A licensed architect for more than twenty years, she had already designed buildings for the Hearsts at the University of California in Berkeley. At San Simeon Morgan (1872–1957) not only designed the Mediterranean-style buildings but also hired the workers and saw that they had good living quarters and even entertainment. Her work ended unfinished in the 1930s, but the fantastic estate, given by the Hearsts to the state, has become one of California's major tourist attractions.

Morgan was born in San Francisco but grew up across the bay in Oakland. For her, if not for her contemporary, Gertrude Stein, there was some "there there." The architect always remained a loyal Californian, even when residing elsewhere. As her biographer, Sara Holmes Boutelle, has written, "Julia herself often remarked on the special advantage of being able to practice architecture in the familiar surroundings of her childhood."

❧ Right. The second-story gables of the Thomas House were probably originally constructed of white stucco, with their eaves painted or stained a darker color. That would link the house to English vernacular architecture, which is more obvious in other houses that Julia Morgan was designing at the same time.

❧ Below. Morgan loved to use heavy, randomly placed boulders on the first floors of her houses, and the porch of the Thomas House is a good example of this technique.

Her undergraduate degree at the University of California was in civil engineering, but she was steered toward architecture by John Galen Howard (1864–1931), the head of the architecture school, and by her friend and teacher, Bernard Maybeck (1862–1957). Apparently Maybeck, who had studied at the Ecole des Beaux-Arts in Paris, encouraged her to go there for professional training. She was the first woman ever to receive a degree from the Ecole. On returning to the Bay Area in 1902, she worked for Howard and then opened her own independent practice in 1904. The earthquake and fire two years later provided plenty of work for her, as it did for other architects.

In the tradition of Beaux-Arts–schooled architects, Morgan could work in almost any style. She even trained her craftspeople to start from a rational plan and work from that—pure Beaux-Arts. For many of her residential structures, however, she adopted the more casual Craftsman mode. Clients in suburban Berkeley, Oakland, and Marin County believed that the woodsy Craftsman style suited the picturesque landscape. How are we to account for this seeming clash with Beaux-Arts formality? Was it just a practical matter of satisfying clients, or did it have some higher purpose? Partly the answer is that for her, as for Maybeck, one style seemed appropriate for public buildings and the other for domestic.

Surely it is not a coincidence that Charles Keeler, spokesman for Maybeck and Berkeley's Hillside Club, was Morgan's university classmate. His little book *The Simple Home* (1904) was extremely influential on house building in the Bay Area. "A simpler, a truer, a more vital art expression is now taking place in California," he observes in the preface. Keeler accepted the Spanish influence on architecture in southern California but found thick adobe walls and deep window reveals out of place in the north. Northern Californians, he said, need "all the sunlight we can get." Casement windows with large panels of glass are necessary in the land of rain and fog, and wood paneling, rafters, and simple furniture clearly expressing its own contruction are appropriate in an area near the redwood forests.

Keeler convinced many Berkeley professors that high thinking would follow from simple living. It was people like these who were Julia Morgan's clients. Anna Thomas was one. Her house in Berkeley became an almost exact manifestation of Keeler's advice.

Hiding behind the plain exterior, the interior is Julia Morgan at her best, which is very good. The entrance hall is small, with an unusually small dining room on the right. The staircase ahead is bold, but the major space is given to the living room to the left. Immediately obvious is Morgan's trademark—crossbeams near the apex of the ceiling. A dressed boulder fireplace catches the eye. The sideboard was probably once in the dining room, given its signs of being cut away from a wall. What looks like a musicians' gallery makes the room even more interesting.

119

❡ It is interesting to compare this straightforward staircase with the one Ernest Coxhead designed for his Freeman House (see page 79). Arranging the dining and living rooms on either side of the central hall was good Beaux-Arts planning. The glass-front sideboard in the living room, not a Morgan design, shows signs of having been moved from the dining room.

❧ Right. With its slatted-wood balcony, the living room is a superb space. Compared to it, the dining room across the hall, with its simple fireplace, is less important.

❧ Opposite. The living room's dressed stone fireplace, with its angled chimney-piece, was a favorite feature of Julia Morgan's houses. Another was the cathedral ceiling with horizontal crossbeams. Board-and-batten walls of redwood make a suitably Craftsman background.

With another nod to the advice of Charles Keeler, who expressed a liking for "burnt wood" sideboards, burnished redwood board-and-batten paneling is everywhere. "An extremely interesting result can be obtained by taking rough sawed boards or timbers and slightly charring the surface," he suggested. "On rubbing this down with sand and an old broom, a soft brown color and interesting wax texture is produced."

Like that of most Arts and Crafts architects, Julia Morgan's oeuvre took a decided turn about 1915. She played with the period revivals, perhaps because she was responding to her clients' wishes, as at San Simeon. But as late as 1939, when asked by Else Schilling to design a Tyrolean country house at Lake Tahoe, Morgan was obviously delighted to design its living room with the boulders and wood paneling that had marked her Craftsman period.

DUNGAN HOUSE

The architectural historian David Gebhard has described John Hudson Thomas's early designs, including the Dungan House, as "the most unbelievable designs to be produced within the Bay Area tradition.... He seems to have gathered on his drafting table a Sweets catalogue of samples of every avant-garde movement which was then being practiced in Europe and America" (*Bay Area Houses*, 1988). Gebhard notes details from the Austrian and German Secessionist movement, Voysey's "Alice in Wonderland cottages," Mackintosh's personal version of Art Nouveau, Wright's Prairie style, America's indigenous Pueblo art, the Mission Revival, and "elements of [Bernard] Maybeck's rich and varied work available right at his doorstep." He adds that Thomas's buildings "are purposely left incomplete, abrupt, awkward, fragmented—impossible." This assessment is somewhat overblown and even wrong in places, but Gebhard is correct in recognizing Thomas's tendency to play games with the Craftsman aesthetic, which was always in danger of becoming quaint or even cute. In the Dungan House, Thomas kept his playfulness under control.

John Hudson Thomas
1911–12 · Berkeley, California

Thomas (1878–1945) was born in Ward, Nevada, where his father was a mining engineer. After an itinerant childhood, in 1902 he was graduated from Yale, his family moved to California, and he began a three-year graduate course in architecture at the University of California in Berkeley. There he studied under two distinguished teachers, Bernard Maybeck (1862–1957) and John Galen Howard (1864–1931). After graduation he worked in Howard's office for two years.

123

❧ Left. Even as it added to the beauty of the place, a stream on the Dungan property made it difficult to construct a house. John Hudson Thomas turned a problem into an asset by using the house to bridge the water, which can be seen from a balcony off the living room.

❧ Below. A front door swathed in vines was the Craftsman way of expressing the relation of architecture to nature. Now well settled into its luxuriant site, the shingled Dungan House looks as if it grew up there as naturally as the trees and foliage.

Although Howard had built his own Craftsman house, he seems to have been of two minds about it. One of his students said that he was scornful of "cottage architecture," and most of his buildings show his Beaux-Arts commitment. Perhaps Thomas found Howard's work too stodgy. Certainly Thomas's record in later years showed his disgust with anything that suggested severe discipline.

In 1906, the year of the great San Francisco earthquake, Thomas formed a partnership with George T. Plowman, another Howard protégé. Many people who had lost homes in the catastrophe decided to rebuild at some distance from the San Andreas Fault, an opportunity for many architects to exploit the disaster and design new houses in Berkeley, Oakland, and Marin County. Thomas and Plowman used this situation to their advantage.

❰ Above. Great banks of mullioned windows, including a clerestory level in the upper reaches, bring plenty of light into the Dungan House. The sedate brick fireplace, a contrasting cave holding the fire's light, rises up equally high to match the windows.

❰ Opposite. In the dining room Thomas boldly used redwood for the built-ins but omitted the usual art glass in the cupboard doors above the sideboard.

The two young architects designed woodsy Craftsman houses that were built mainly in Berkeley. Their designs fitted well into the notion of building with nature espoused by the Hillside Club, a cultural institution made up largely of people connected with the university and strongly devoted to the view that Berkeley was a special place. The Chisholm House (ca. 1907), for example, had all the wood siding and pergolas needed to make it harmonize with a Maybeck house nearby. Probably Plowman was the enthusiast for this style; after 1910, when their partnership was dissolved, Thomas was much more adventuresome, showing that he was conversant with many styles even as he played tricks with them.

Hubert Leo Dungan and his wife, Edda, liked Maybeck, who had often shown people the couple's existing Craftsman house in Berkeley. It was assumed that when they needed a larger house, they would hire him as their architect. The story is that when the Dungans showed Maybeck the sketches that Leo had drawn, the architect said that they did not need him. Realizing that he in fact needed help, Leo then called on Thomas, who accepted their commission and drew the plans in April 1911.

The Dungans' picturesque site, actually two lots, had a number of magnificent trees planted in the mid-nineteenth century and a brook running through the property. Thomas made the house a bridge over the stream, which flows out under a balcony off the living room—a Craftsman Fallingwater. He also translated the Tudor style, apparently his clients' choice, into high-pitched roofs and gables sprouting quaint dormers. According to Robert Judson Clark, "Maybeck is there, but don't forget Ernest Coxhead, whose Beta Theta Pi fraternity house (1893–94) is not far away. Thomas could not possibly have missed that and other Coxhead buildings."

As in most Craftsman houses, wood abounds. The exteriors of the living room wing and first floor of the main house are covered with redwood shakes a yard long with a twenty-inch overlap. The Tudor black-and-white work on the second, attic story has its own exposed timbers. The interior too is woodsy. The front hall, living room, and dining room are paneled in redwood board and batten and have exposed ceiling beams. All the floors are made of two-inch tongue-and-groove hardwood. Maybeck's spirit hovers over this house in features such as the sudden explosion of space.

At the same time that Thomas was designing the Dungan House, he was supervising construction on his Locke House (1911) in Oakland, an incredible mixture of American Mission Revival and Austrian Secessionism, neither holding up very well under attack from the other. But soon he simmered down into more conventional interpretations of period revival styles. After 1915 Thomas and American architecture in general fell into the trap of superficiality. The season of expressive creativity came to an end.

127

❦ Redwood board-and-batten paneling, a favorite Craftsman expression, covers the walls of the Dungan House staircase. A large bank of windows ushers light into what might have been a dark space. The handsome built-in cabinet is a perfect place to store children's toys.

THE CLOSE

The Close seems to be the only house in the United States designed by Mackay Hugh Baillie Scott (1865–1945), the son of a wealthy Scottish laird. Although the family had the means to send him to Oxford or Cambridge, he received his higher education at the Cirencester Agricultural College largely because his father wanted him to manage his sheep ranches in Australia. After graduation Scott, belatedly acknowledging his artistic bent, decided to become an architect instead of a farmer. At the time England had no architecture schools, so in the British tradition he was articled (apprenticed) to the city architect of Bath. When he had learned as much as he could, he set up an independent practice on the Isle of Man, where he designed half-timbered houses in what was then called the "Old English" style.

Conventional on the exterior, his houses inside exhibited his passion for interconnecting spaces separated by screens that could be folded up, leaving a large arena for a dance or a party. In 1909 Scott described such an interior in the journal *Studio:* "[T]o get some idea of its general effect I must transport you to some old Cheshire farm house, somewhere in the country where people have not yet grown to be ashamed of plain bricks and whitewash."

Such strange ideas expanded when Scott developed an ornamental streak. The exteriors of his houses might remain simple, understated wattle-and-daub, but the interiors took on a richness of decoration that, despite his professed devotion to William Morris's ideals of simplicity, were very close to being decadent.

It was this ornamental indulgence that attracted the Grand Duke of Hesse, Ernst Ludwig, to Scott's work. In 1897 the duke commissioned the architect to design some rooms in his palace at Darmstadt, Germany, near Stuttgart. At the same time he engaged C. R. Ashbee (1863–1942), another disciple of William Morris, to create the interiors. What followed was an inspired collaboration: Scott was responsible for the designs and the ornament, while the furniture and other appointments were executed by Ashbee's Guild and School of Handicraft. The result was widely published and led to many commissions for Scott. It also prompted Ernst Ludwig to summon other architects—Peter Behrens and Joseph Maria Olbrich, among others—to Darmstadt to create an Arts and Crafts–Jugendstil colony that, with some reconstruction since World War II, still exists.

This high style, well published in the *International Studio*, lasted only a while. Scott's later work was much less spirited, but as he gave up excess, he restored the Arts and Crafts ideal of fine craftsmanship just at the time that many architects, such as Edwin Lutyens (1869–1944), were adopting neoclassicism or the neo-Georgian mode.

❦ With its half-timbered stucco finish, The Close epitomizes the English variant of the Arts and Crafts style—a not-unexpected choice given the architect's main body of work in Britain. A picturesque side entrance, set into a two-story gabled bay, opens into the garden.

❡ Above. The Close's main entrance is tucked away on the side, beneath a second-story oriel projecting outward to offer shelter.

❡ Right. The rear courtyard is particularly characteristic of Scott's "Old English" style. Window treatments show his debt to the English architect C.F.A. Voysey. A brick chimney looms above the tiled roof.

❡ Opposite, top left. The no-nonsense lines of Stickley furnishings suit The Close, Scott's only American commission. Stickley used machines, however, to create the hand-crafted feel espoused by William Morris, the architect's countryman.

❡ Opposite, top right. Casement windows are dressed up with elaborate hardware, producing a lively transition from rectilinear to curvilinear shapes. Stickley himself would have approved these homespun pillows with their embroidered nature motifs.

❡ Opposite, bottom left. A built-in window seat, framed by rich chestnut paneling, ties The Close to Arts and Crafts homes on both sides of the Atlantic.

❡ Opposite, bottom right. The beautiful chestnut woodwork and contrasting papered walls act as a warm backdrop for the dining room's Stickley furniture. The beamed ceiling and handcrafted door pull add to The Close's English medieval flavor.

❡ Below. One of several dormers helps light a hallway in the large Craftsman house, which rises two and one-half stories.

In spite of its size, large as American houses go, The Close is a marvelous example of Scott's joy in the nature of materials, in this case wood. The house is framed in nine-inch-thick chestnut timbers that are revealed in the exterior's Tudor-derived black-and-white work. The client, Henry Binsse, had asked that the house look like an old English inn. Scott obliged him—except that it is much bigger than an inn was likely to be in seventeenth-century England.

Except for the living room, the interior spaces are small but rich in chestnut paneling and other woodwork; they apparently were never intended to have the fussy decoration of Scott's earlier houses. He commissioned McKim, Mead and White as supervising American architects of the house, and the firm carried out his plans in immaculate detail. The finished product with its white walls and beamed ceilings is a fine backdrop for the present owner's Stickley furniture.

In 1925 John D. Clarke, an admirer of Scott's architecture, wrote:

Can we with our modern machine-made materials and machine-like labour hope to produce as satisfying work as was produced before machinery came to curse or bless us? Mr. Baillie Scott says "No." His answer is: "A study of old building one finds in . . . villages, suggests that it is not only better than any modern building, but has some essential difference. . . . This difference largely consists in the character of the workmanship which, like handwriting, conveys personality instead of being a lifeless mechanical formula."

The Close never achieved the notoriety of Scott's elaborate interiors published in the *International Studio* and other journals; it was, rather, much more in line with the American Craftsman aesthetic that discouraged ornament in favor of fine craftsmanship. Although almost unknown to most American architectural historians, it remains not only a rare English intrusion in the American Arts and Crafts movement but also an example of the embodiment of William Morris's principle of simplicity—on a large scale.

133

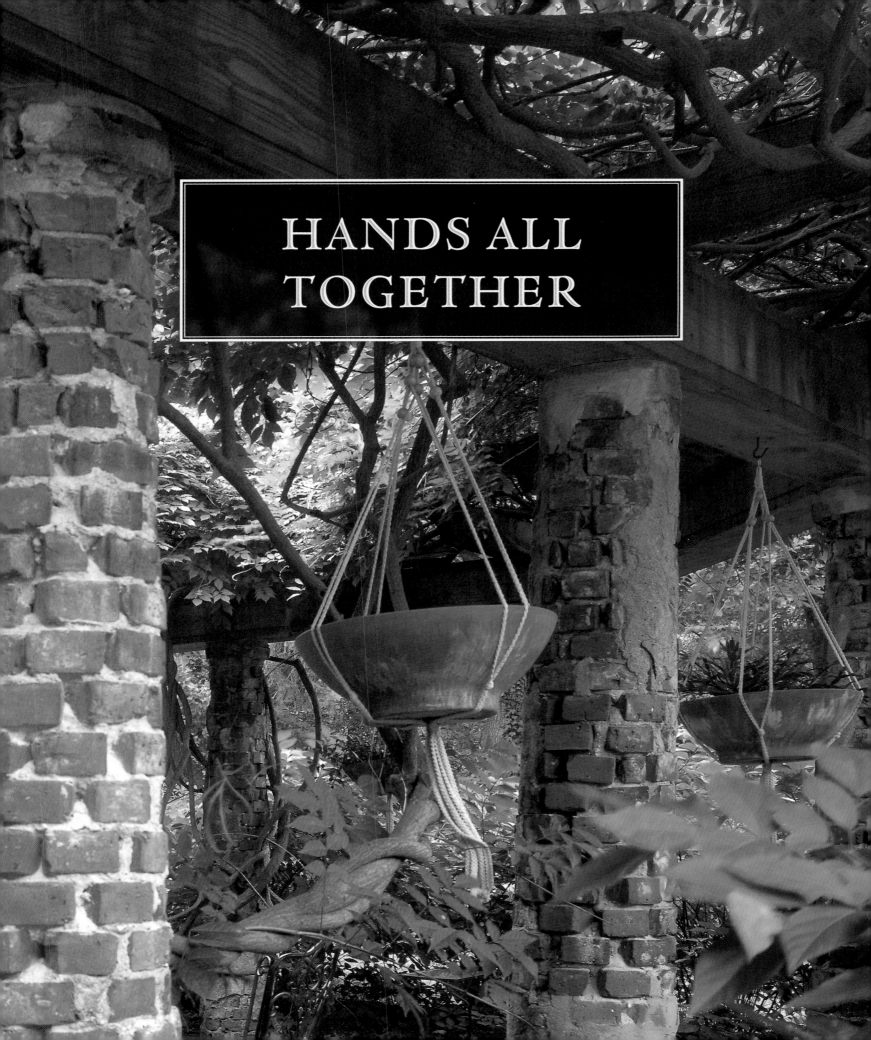

HANDS ALL
TOGETHER

ROYCROFT COLONY

History has not been kind to Elbert Hubbard (1856–1915), once called the "Sage of East Aurora." A former soap salesman and a failed novelist, he was drawn to the ideas of William Morris, which he attempted to emulate by founding his own community of artisans, the Roycroft Colony in East Aurora, New York, near Buffalo. It included the Roycroft Press, a pale imitation of Morris's Kelmscott Press, and an inspirational magazine, *The Philistine* (1895–1915), "whose platitudinously 'arty' content was mainly written by himself," according to *The Oxford Companion to American Literature* (1965).

Although not taken very seriously in his day—who could take seriously someone who so often laughed at himself?—Hubbard was appreciated as a person worth knowing. Stephen Crane was a guest at the Roycroft Inn, which Hubbard opened in 1900 to attract notables.

Elbert Hubbard · 1896–1915
East Aurora, New York

The poet Richard Hovey, whom Hubbard "carried thru three hard winters," was finally banished because he would not churn butter. Richard le Galliene spent two summers at the colony. Frank Lloyd Wright, an old friend, sat on the inn's front porch and talked art with Hubbard; in fact, Wright's cravat, pork-pie hat, and even his logo, the red square, were derived directly from Hubbard's regalia.

Hubbard was born in Bloomington, Illinois, and grew up there. His sister married John Larkin, a Chicago soap manufacturer who gave Elbert a job selling soap in the Midwest. When Larkin set up a new factory in Buffalo, Elbert went along and proved to be an excellent salesman (he probably helped Wright get the commission for his famous Larkin Administration Building of 1903). In 1884 Hubbard was able to buy a large house in East Aurora within commuting distance of Buffalo. He also invested in the Larkin Company and, when he sold his stock in 1892, had accumulated a small fortune. He applied for admission to Harvard, which found his educational background inadequate but accepted him as a special student; he did not last long there.

137

Hubbard then traveled to Europe and began writing *Little Journeys* (1895–1909) about his visits to the houses of famous people. Seeing the home of William Morris seems to have given him the idea of creating an Arts and Crafts community in East Aurora. By 1896 he was advertising it as a place for anyone who would come. Some, mostly young, did.

❰ Left. The 1899 chapel, built with local boulders as a meeting place rather than a religious building, is now the East Aurora town hall. Janet Ashbee found a "Brook Farm feeling" to the colony.

❰ Right. The Print Shop (1900) housed the presses that printed Hubbard's books and his magazine, *The Philistine*, which served as a platform for his causes and aphorisms.

 Above. Art glass windows in the old part of the Roycroft Inn, created in 1900 from the former print shop, were designed by the noted Arts and Crafts artist Dard Hunter (1883–1958), who was obviously well acquainted with Mackintosh and Austrian Secessionism. This one is on the staircase.

  Right. Roycroft's library is capped by a welter of exposed beams—the "stickwork" often required of Arts and Crafts interiors.

 Below. At one time this chandelier, also designed by Dard Hunter, hung on the porch of the old Roycroft Inn. He was the kind of artist that Janet Ashbee thought Elbert Hubbard needed but who appeared on the scene only after she had visited.

In 1900 Janet Ashbee, the wife of C. R. Ashbee (1863–1942), the English reformer and follower of William Morris, visited Hubbard while her husband was on a lecture tour in the United States. Mrs. Ashbee, although amused by Hubbard, admired his venture. She described the workshops, constructed of stone that Hubbard had purchased from local farmers at a dollar a load: "Great bits of purple and brown and grey, put crudely together by the Roycrofters who keep their buildings living near as the mediaeval folks did, and in the intervals of book-making lend a hand to spread mortar or to adjust a corner stone." Ashbee noted that the apparent source of income for the experiment in communal craftsmanship came from *The Philistine*, subscriptions to which were a dollar a year. *The Philistine*, she said, "amply pays wages, prints books, makes gardens, produces excellent carpenter work, and a little good smithing, and enables a delightful crank to run what appears to be an ideal community. If he also makes good profits, who's to blame him?"

Her observations on the work produced by the Roycroft Colony—its books, ironwork, leather goods, and furniture—are incisive:

In the Library he has some . . . specimens of Roycroft binding, poor stuff most of it, but wonderful considering the 5 years only of growth. He has 8 or 10 presses worked by a gas engine, and one little forlorn hand press that he uses for pulling special proofs. What the place lacks is someone with a strong instinct of beauty—who will refuse to pass those inorganic designs, and the colours that fight. At present they go on the "do it as well as you can" principle which is very human; but they turn out a lot of poor work.

In the little forge, which smelt of home, they were making some hideous gas brackets, great unconstructional things, just for the want of knowing the first principles of design. And those tables and chairs of theirs were good.

To Hubbard's rueful comment that he was locally considered a heretic, Ashbee responded: "His heresy seems pretty sound though; mostly Ruskin and Morris with a good strong American flavour." His experiment in creating an American Arts and Crafts community all but collapsed when he and his wife went down with the *Luisitania* in 1915. His chapter ended at just about the time the movement itself waned in significance.

❧ Above. A bookcase in the Roycroft Museum brings to mind an Arts and Crafts dictum of Charles Keeler in *The Simple Home* (1904): "Masses of books have an ornamental value which is heightened by the idea of culture of which they are the embodiment."

❧ Opposite. A medallion of William Morris graces a split-stone fireplace made from local boulders. The seahorse andirons (see also page 44) were made by the Roycrofters.

❧ Below. An exhibition of Roycroft wares now occupies the museum's dining room.

ROSE VALLEY AND ARDEN

The Craftsman communities of Arden and Rose Valley were founded by a group of socially conscious friends, all of whom lived in Philadelphia. They included the soap manufacturers Joseph and Samuel Fels, the *Ladies' Home Journal* publisher Edward Bok, and John Gilmore, a wealthy financier. But the designer and principal figure of both settlements was William Lightfoot Price (1861–1916), well known as an enormously successful designer of houses for the rich but who had remained a liberal interested in society's less fortunate. His vision of an ideal community was a place where "the tiniest cottages may be built side by side with a more spacious neighbor."

Will Price · 1900–1901
Rose Valley, Pennsylvania
Arden, Delaware

Naturally the ideas of William Morris appealed to Price. Both Rose Valley and Arden were intended to be Arts and Crafts colonies, but a related reform movement with a more material impulse was behind their founding. One of Price's friends boasted that he had converted him "to the religion of Henry George." George (1839–97) was an economist whose single-tax theory was accepted by his followers as divinely inspired. Now dismissed as a tinkerer, George was taken very seriously in the late nineteenth and early twentieth centuries by such important figures as George Bernard Shaw, Sun Yat-sen, John Dewey, and Leo Tolstoy. When C. R. Ashbee (1863–1942), one of the great British Arts and Crafts practitioners, visited the Pasadena architect Charles Greene in 1909, he described ending the day at Greene's house on the Arroyo Seco: "We looked out on the mountains and discussed single tax in the intervals of tea and fingering the surfaces of Greene's scholarly paneling."

142

❦ Right. An art glass window created by Nicola D'Ascenzo for the front door of Rose Hedge hints at the Scottish rose made famous by Charles Rennie Mackintosh while it signifies Rose Valley itself. The community's own symbol was a wild rose with a superimposed V for Valley.

❦ Opposite. Will Price's older brother, Walter F. Price, built Rose Hedge in 1906, converting it from an old farmhouse into a home for himself and his new bride, Felicia. With its Tuscan red tile roof, stucco walls, and airy pergola, it served as a prototype for a later home of his.

❦ Below. When Rose Valley's artisans took over the Old Mill as their furniture shop, they built a stone bridge over Vernon Run to beautify their pathway between work and home.

❧ Left. Thunderbird Lodge, the Rose Valley house that Will Price converted in 1904 for the artists Alice Barber Stephens and her husband, Charles Hallowell Stephens, is almost without conscious style. "It is what it was intended to be," Price declared, "the home and workshop of busy artists, and the grounds and gardens growing up around it are the simple and direct character that might be expected to result from the old environment and the new life growing up within it." The lodge was originally the barn to the farmhouse that became Rose Hedge.

❧ Above. A colorful masonry mix enlivens the house's first floor and porch columns.

❧ Right. Thunderbird Lodge's Gothic windows take in a wide swath of nature, which in Rose Valley includes heavily wooded lots bisected by streams, ponds, and bridges.

George's social conscience—he was concerned with why there was so much poverty in the midst of plenty—complemented the theories of John Ruskin and William Morris. As a young man he had visited Calcutta and was revolted by the suffering of the poor. His concern was deepened by a stay in New York City in the winter of 1868–69, where he observed "the shocking contrast between monstrous wealth and debasing want." Without denying the right to private property, he advocated taxing away the "unearned increment" that property owners, through no effort of their own, received from the natural increase in property values. George argued that a single tax on the value of property was all that was needed to raise revenue to bring social services to all the people. This solution, although perhaps simplistic, seemed to many people in the Progressive Era an idea worth trying. George's finest book, *Progress and Poverty* (1879), sold more than two million copies in the United States alone.

In 1901 Price bought eighty acres of land along the Delaware River near the Philadelphia suburb of Media. What became Rose Valley was located in one of the many hollows where mills and factories had operated in the early days of industrialization, when waterpower moved the machinery. As production relocated to the cities where steam power was available, the old factories fell into disrepair and were abandoned. Rose Valley had its own ruined mill. What better place could be found to restore the handicraft tradition than where industry seemed to have failed?

❴ Left. Thunderbird Lodge in Rose Valley is entered through an open reception area separated from the living room by a wide segmental arch and low walls that act as a subtle gate.

147

❴ Below. The fireplace mantel in Charles Stephens's studio at Thunderbird Lodge once held part of the couple's collection of American Indian objects, which inspired the name of the house. The broad stone arch mirrors the doorway between the living room and the entry.

Rose Valley's history parallels that of C. R. Ashbee's similar experiment at Chipping Campden in the English Cotswolds, which occurred at almost exactly the same time. Price had visited Ashbee's Guild and School of Handicraft when it was located in East London and knew of Ashbee's intention to move it to the country. Both Ashbee's enterprise and Price's colony were partly financed by Joseph Fels, both soon fell into financial difficulties, and both had broken up by 1910.

Rose Valley was supposed to have been a haven for furniture makers, potters, metalsmiths, and other crafts workers who were to settle into the old millworkers' cottages, but only the furniture shop, under the direct supervision of Price and Hawley McLanahan (1865–1929), another Philadelphia architect who moved into the colony in 1905, amounted to anything. Extremely expensive and somewhat odd, the furniture was called "Gothic" because it resembled the pulpit and communion-table style built for Gothic Revival churches. A visitor from the U.S. Bureau of Labor described its means of construction:

Glue is very little used, and is never depended on for strength. Chair backs are cut out of solid wood, table tops are double dovetailed, and no attempt is made to conceal joints or pegs. The grain of the wood is carefully selected for the particular use to which the wood is to be put, and free use is made of carving by way of ornament. The result is handsome and expensive furniture, the prices depending upon the time employed in making particular pieces.

❲ Above. To cover the community's debts, speculative houses were designed for the Rose Valley Improvement Company using stucco, stone, and hollow tile. Artisans could not afford houses of this scale.

❲ Opposite, top left. Inset tiles were used like confetti to dress up plain stucco walls on houses as well as community markers.

❲ Opposite, top right. This Mercer tile was probably a special order to commemorate the namesake of Rose Valley.

❲ Opposite, bottom left. John Maene, the chief furniture carver, made this double Gothic bench in Rose Valley's Old Mill.

❲ Opposite, bottom right. At Will Price's own house, originally the grist mill manager's home, the curved concrete fireplace is inset with Mercer tiles forming three V's.

Opposite. In a 1913 Arden cottage named The Burgage that backs up to Sherwood Forest (Arden Forest is on the opposite side of town), a heavily mortared fireplace with a wood mantel offers a warm refuge.

Bottom left. At The Burgage's ornately decorated Craftsman door, guests are welcomed but warned not to stay too long.

Bottom right. Among Arden's mix of early-twentieth-century house styles, The Burgage's shingled California bungalow style looks right at home. Its shed roof dormer, bringing light into the attic, clearly ties it to Craftsman bungalows.

Not far from Rose Valley, just outside Wilmington, Delaware, Henry George's theory gave birth to the community of Arden, where a form of the single tax is still used today. After attempts to change Delaware's tax assessment methods were roundly foiled, Price joined with the sculptor G. Frank Stephens (1859–1935) to start an independent Georgist colony. "We had learned William Morris' truth that nothing can be done for Art until we have bridged the terrible gulf between the rich and the poor," Stephens recalled in 1923. He purchased a farm in 1900, and the founders, having practiced Shakespeare to hone their oratorical skills in furtherance of their cause, named their new garden city Arden, after the Forest of Arden in *As You Like It*. Aiming to attract craftsmen, artists, musicians, and other utopian dreamers, Price laid out a model village ringed by woodland and with a town green and plenty of parks, encouraging residents to craft their own homes.

Price's architecture in Rose Valley as well as in Arden is fascinating in light of the fact that he had been building mansions for the rich in Gothic and Chateauesque modes. His most important houses in Rose Valley—the McLanahan House, designed in a curious blend of the English vernacular Arts and Crafts Voysey style and the wavy lines of Art Nouveau (which Price said "has a good substantial kick to it"), and Thunderbird Lodge for Alice and Charles Hallowell Stephens—were Price's interpretations of English Arts and Crafts houses: Voyseyesque for the McLanahans, English vernacular for the Stephenses. Price's designs for the architecture of Arden were conservative: versions of the English vernacular Tudor and cottage styles, much in the vein of his Rose Valley houses.

Besides Price's houses, furniture, and other artifacts, one other record of the Rose Valley experiment remains—a journal, *The Artsman*, published between October 1903 and April 1907. The title itself indicates a desire to complement Gustav Stickley's *The Craftsman*. Its editor, Horace Traubel, a friend of Walt Whitman, never moved to Rose Valley, however. While he wrote articles on the Rose Valley experiment and illustrated them with quaint drawings, he remained in Philadelphia. Arden has published its own monthly for a century. Today Rose Valley is a picturesque suburban enclave, while Arden perhaps fulfills its promise of an egalitarian Arts and Crafts colony better now than when it was founded. So popular was it that Henry George's legacy has been extended to two adjacent settlements: Ardentown, established in 1922, and Ardencroft, which followed in 1950.

❦ Opposite. At Green Gate, built in Arden in 1909, a dining room frieze captures a Dutch tavern scene. It was painted about 1915 by Buzz Ware, a prominent local artist whose mother was a founder of the American Communist Party. The pots at left are Niloak Mission Ware.

❦ Below. For Green Gate and other buildings at Arden, Will Price leaned toward Tudor rather than Rose Valley's plainer style.

152

❦ Right. Frank Stephens's first home was a one-room cabin, but for its 1909 replacement, a simplified Tudor called the Second Homestead, he moved to the Arden Green. Close by, an outdoor theater named in his honor maintains Arden's theatrical roots.

❦ Above. The storybook cottage, with its twin Hansel and Gretel gables, has medieval windows and a corner Gothic sculpture, undoubtedly the sculptor's work.

BYRDCLIFFE

Ralph Radcliffe Whitehead
1902–5
Woodstock, New York

Arts and Crafts proponents, beginning with John Ruskin and William Morris, looked backward to a better day (despite the contrary proclamation on Frank Stephens's house in Arden). Machines had enslaved humankind, they believed, and they vowed to fight modernization. The Craftsman movement, prone to inventing a history that never existed, extolled a quiet past—"an epoch of rest," as Morris put it. Is it any wonder that it produced a few eccentrics? Charles Lummis, Elbert Hubbard, Henry Mercer, and even William Morris himself were oddities; Ralph Radcliffe Whitehead could definitely be classified as an eccentric.

Whitehead (1854–1929), the son of a wealthy textile manufacturer in Yorkshire, England, was of conventional, bourgeois stock. A graduate of Balliol College at Oxford, he had studied with John Ruskin, whom he had accompanied on a visit to Venice in 1876. He accepted both Ruskin's theory that the Renaissance had ushered in a time of troubles and his professor's antimodernist philosophy. Initially enthusiastic about Ruskin's Guild of St. George, intended to liberate people from the worst aspects of the machine age, Whitehead became critical of it when its utopias failed. However, Ruskin's concept of cooperative communities was behind the founding of Byrdcliffe in New York State in 1902.

Having inherited his father's large fortune, Whitehead was free to engage in experiments. After one failed marriage, he courted Jane Byrd McCall, a Philadelphia debutante who was also a cousin of the tilemaker Henry Mercer. In 1891, before they were married, they swore allegiance to a contract committing themselves to Arts and Crafts ideals—a fealty more binding, as far as Whitehead was concerned, than their marriage vows the following year. They built a house, Arcady, in Santa Barbara, California, covering the walls with William Morris wallpapers and filling it with the works of C.F.A. Voysey and other English craftspeople. Jane at first thought the house too big but grew to love it, refusing to leave it even when her husband began his wanderings, geographical and amorous.

❦ Below and opposite. Whitehead called his house at Byrdcliffe White Pines because the site reminded him of a scene in Walter Pater's *Marius the Epicurean* (1885), in which a farm in his beloved Umbria is called White Nights. He never forgot his Italian travels with Ruskin.

Whitehead was obsessed with the idea of creating an Arts and Crafts community where all the arts—painting, sculpture, and music as well as ceramics, metalwork, and furniture making—would have a home. His attempt to establish such a community near Albany, Oregon, failed because of internal bickering. Why he did not attempt one in Santa Barbara, where there were already talented crafts workers and a benevolent climate in which to work, is unclear.

In 1901, while on a trip to Chicago to investigate a lifelong interest in extrasensory perception, he met Hervey White, a Harvard graduate who had studied with Charles Eliot Norton and had been converted to the Arts and Crafts theory of this friend of Ruskin. The same year Bolton Brown, chair of the art department at Stanford University, appeared on Whitehead's doorstep in Santa Barbara on an ultimately successful mission to sell him Japanese prints.

Together the three new friends—White, Brown, and Whitehead—scouted the East Coast for a suitable site for an Arts and Crafts colony. Probably at Jane Whitehead's insistence, her husband and White searched the South as well for a likely spot. Brown, a native New Yorker, proposed the town of Woodstock in the Catskills, which seemed to meet all of Whitehead's specifications, including the fact that at that time it had almost no Jews (Whitehead was an outspoken anti-Semite). The choice had an odd resonance: the Catskills were soon to become a playground for New York's Jewish bourgeoisie. At Woodstock, Whitehead found the fresh air and scenery that he desired. He called the location Byrdcliffe, a merging of his and Jane's middle names.

❧ Opposite. Jane Whitehead's cousin Henry Mercer, founder of the Moravian Pottery and Tile Works in Pennsylvania, made the tiles for the fireplace surround in the living hall of White Pines at Byrdcliffe.

❧ Below. After 1916, a decade following the demise of the Byrdcliffe colony, Ralph and Jane Whitehead turned out a great deal of pottery in the attic of White Pines.

❦ Above. This is a simple but fine built-in bench and dresser in one of the bedrooms at White Pines, which is incomplete largely because Jane Whitehead refused to live there until 1905. By then the Byrdcliffe colony had pretty much closed down.

❦ Right. A kind of "bridge of sighs" connects the main house to the loom room, where the Whiteheads wove cloth à la William Morris.

❦ Below. Ralph Whitehead set cabins for artists in the lovely Catskills landscape. Given fanciful names such as Morning Glory, Fleur-de-lys, Carniola, and Eastover (shown), the wooden cottages apparently were never intended to be year-round dwellings.

Envisioning a summer retreat for artists and intellectuals, all financed by his own great fortune, Whitehead began to build about thirty-five buildings to house the artists he intended to attract. The buildings have a southern California bungalow stylelessness about them with just a touch of Swiss chalet, as befits a summer camp. Most of the artists came as teachers to Whitehead's summer school and then pursued their crafts on the side, with the result that little of their output can be associated directly with Byrdcliffe.

Easily the finest work produced at Byrdcliffe was the furniture. A number of artists contributed to it, but it has a distinct Byrdcliffe style: almost Shaker-like in the simplicity of its construction but often decorated with delicate, low bas-relief panels featuring skillfully carved flowers and leaves indigenous to the Catskills against an orange-stained background. The result was exquisite—and very expensive—work. Much of the furniture that was made, about fifty pieces, remained inside White Pines, the Whiteheads' house at Byrdcliffe, after their deaths. Some of it is stamped "Byrdcliffe 1904," although not all of it could have been built that year.

By 1905 the colony had pretty much closed down. Jane and Ralph dabbled in pottery and entertained famous guests such as C. R. Ashbee. After Whitehead's death in 1929, Jane ran the colony as the summer retreat it had been designed to be. The clientele ranged far beyond craftspeople, including at one time or another John Dewey, Charlotte Perkins Gilman, Thomas Mann, Helen Hayes, Milton Avery, Bob Dylan, and Chevy Chase. Woodstock remains an artists' colony, although hardly the Craftsman utopia that Ralph Whitehead envisioned.

❨ Above. The fireplace in Byrdcliffe's loom room has a Greek inscription—ΧΑΡΙΣ ΧΑΡΙΝ ΓΑΡ ΕΣΤΙΝ Η ΤΙΚΤΟΥΣ ΑΕΙ—from line 522 of Sophocles' *Ajax*: "Kindness return of kindness 'er begets." The sculpture is the *Nike of Samothrace,* without wings. Over it hangs a detail from Botticelli's *Birth of Venus.*

❨ Opposite. A tiny model of a loom emphasizes Whitehead's interest in fabrics. The pots were designed and thrown at Byrdcliffe, possibly by one of the Whiteheads.

BUNGALOW HEAVEN

In various American cities—Chicago, Minneapolis, Seattle, Dallas, and Washington, D.C., for example—bungalows of the early twentieth century are still sought after as pleasant, affordable places to live, and throughout the country organizations devoted to their preservation and enjoyment have sprung up. But nowhere is this one- or one-and-one-half-story, single-family house with enough land for a small garden more venerated than in southern California. The movement even has its own magazine, *American Bungalow*. This admiration is deserved: in the history of architecture, the bungalow is the only house type created for common people that was produced in any quantity and that had style. It was usually, at least in the first two decades of the century, the woodsy Craftsman style. From 1920 to 1930, the period during which most bungalows were built, however, these usually small houses were fashioned in almost every conceivable historical mode.

Mostly pre-1920
Pasadena, California

Pasadena's Bungalow Heaven, in the northeast section of the city, was developed mostly before 1920 and except for a few intrusions is a remarkably coherent community, having somehow escaped the worst onslaughts of modern developers, freeway builders, and agents of mansionization. Twenty-nine square blocks of bungalows have been officially designated a city historic district.

Bungalow Heaven is in the best sense a bourgeois community. Although the district is near gang-infested areas, there are practically no crime or drug problems. The houses are kept painted or stained, and the trees, bushes, and lawns are trimmed, in some cases to perfection. Some are furnished with Craftsman pieces. Ironically, the original owners probably would not have been able to afford Stickley's tables and chairs. Their inclusion in these bungalows is a reflection of the present owners' higher income and their taste for simple but exquisitely built furniture. The result is a vision—not an authentic representation—of the past through contemporary eyes.

What is authentic about these bungalows is that they, on their small plots, continue to represent the traditional American idea of home: a single-family house set in a garden, however small. In the eighteenth and nineteenth centuries they were associated with resorts or, as in India, were built in compounds outside cities. Always they were retreats from the urban environment—and urban problems. A further irony is that, with the coming of the streetcar and the automobile in the early twentieth century, the bungalow was urbanized, allowing people to live at a distance from their workplace and the heart of the city yet enjoy the fruits of urbanity. For a time bungalows, usually heavily mortgaged, fulfilled the dream of the working classes as well as the young and the elderly. Often they were thought of as temporary homes, but many people found them so agreeable that they became permanent residences.

165

◖ One of Pasadena's finest bungalow courts, Gartz Court was developed about 1915 by Kate Gartz, a rich socialist, as an example of proper housing for workers. The idea for such courts may have come from the positioning of cabins at tuberculosis sanitariums.

The California bungalow evolved during the Craftsman period, typically using an amalgam of Japanese and Swiss motifs—with a little Tudor thrown in. Although small, they had a tendency to spread out over a property; thus a bungalow not only was expensive to construct but also required a lot of land. Compared to other parts of the country, land in California was cheap. Elsewhere the average frontage of a lot was approximately thirty to thirty-five feet; in California it was characteristically fifty or more feet.

As the cost of land increased, developers sought ways to use space more efficiently. The eventual result was the apartment house, but before 1920 the solution was to fit a house to smaller pieces of property. Another solution, a California invention found less often in other parts of the country, was the bungalow court—a grouping of bungalows, usually in a U shape around a central court sometimes containing a fountain. The idea was to squeeze a number of houses into a relatively small lot. As a result these bungalows were even smaller than usual.

The first known bungalow court was the St. Francis Court (1909) in Pasadena, designed by the local architect Sylvanus Marston (1883–1946) for Frank D. Hogan, a developer, to attract winter visitors. These bungalows were not intended for the poor. Elegant in their Craftsman woodsiness, they were furnished with Stickley furniture, oriental and Navajo rugs, and other fine appointments; some even had quarters for a maid.

The idea was adopted by other developers. In 1910 Irving Gill designed Lewis Court in nearby Sierra Madre, and the same year Arthur and Alfred Heineman, always close to developers if not actually engaged in development themselves,

❧ Tree-lined streets in Pasadena's Bungalow Heaven are filled with well-designed and well-maintained bungalows such as these. Residents still sit on their front porches and, as Jane Jacobs would phrase it, patrol the street with their eyes.

❧ Opposite, top. An über Craftsman bungalow dining room in the home of Kennon Miedema and Julie Reiz centers around the built-in buffet with art glass doors and a mirrored back that visually expands the space.

❧ Opposite, bottom. Tile in the fireplace surround, suggesting leaves fallen to earth, offers a contrast to the wood marking the mantel and built-in bookcase. Above them, molding enbraces the windows as part of the same woodsy ensemble.

designed Bowen Court in Pasadena (see page 27). Intended for people of modest means, the complex of twenty-three tiny bungalows was much simpler than St. Francis Court, but its location among palms and oaks was pure California picturesque.

The bungalow court had at least one important detractor. Charles Sumner Greene (1868–1957), who worked best with rich clients, wrote in *The Architect* in 1915: "The bungalow court idea is to be regretted." Bowen Court, he observed, "would seem to have no other reason for being than that of making money for the investor. The style and design of each unit is uniform, making for the monotony and dreariness of a factory district. Added to this, the buildings are hopelessly crowded." And he ended with emphasis, "This is a good example of what not to do."

Today a different point of view prevails. Many of these bungalow courts have been turned into offices, offering a humanizing quality to commercial space. Moreover, the bungalow court provided the model for that phenomenon of American travel history, the motel of the 1920s.

Unfortunately, because bungalows were the houses of lower-middle-class and blue-collar workers, they were endangered by economic downturns. Many people lost theirs in the Great Depression of the 1930s, and many more would have had it not been for the passage of a New Deal law that offered loans for homeowners. Even so, by 1930 the great period of bungalow building had passed. The bungalow type was revived after World War II, but the term *bungalow* was rarely applied to the house types that followed the war: Cape Cod cottages, ranch houses, and tract houses. Architecture once again became the exclusive property of the rich and well born.

❈ Left. Stickwork in this pair of gables in Pasadena's Bungalow Heaven underscores the Arts and Crafts movement's thesis that architectural honesty arose from clear structural expression. Natural colors and materials link the bungalow to the earth.

❈ Below. Front doors of bungalows came in a variety of styles. With its symmetrical sidelights, this one carries a faint touch of the Classical Revival. The flattened arch is repeated indoors, over the entry to the dining room and in the room's woodwork, including the built-in buffet.

❲ Above. What looks like a built-in cabinet hides not just a desk but also a stowaway bed—a real space saver in a small bungalow.

❲ Left. A flattened archway recalling the front door calls attention to what is typically the most elaborate room in any bungalow: the dining room. Board-and-batten wainscoting rises on either side of the elaborate built-in buffet and encircles the room to envelop diners in the wood tones of a forest.

IN THE
PUBLIC REALM

MISSION INN

❦ Opposite. A part of the original building, The Cloister (1911) by Arthur Benton, is in the foreground, beginning at the first buttress. The domed tower is said to have been inspired by the Carmel Mission, while the buttresses were modeled on those at the San Gabriel Mission.

❦ Below left. Even Charles Fletcher Lummis, a close friend of Frank Miller, made his way frequently to Riverside. The woman standing by the registration desk as Lummis signs in is Alice Richardson, Miller's sister, who for many years was the inn's manager.

❦ Below right. The music room in the Mission Inn's original Cloister wing is one of the few spaces that remain as they once looked.

Originally a family residence that was expanded about 1876 into a boarding house and later a small hotel, the Mission Inn today covers an entire city block. Why it became so popular in the period 1902 to 1930 and even why it was built in the first place—about fifty miles from the burgeoning metropolis of Los Angeles—are questions that remain to tantalize historians. Even in the hotel's heyday, 1923, Riverside had a population of only about 26,000, Yet despite many remodelings and setbacks along the way, it still dazzles.

The inn's first manager was Frank Miller, a local boy who in 1880, for five thousand dollars, bought the small but sound enterprise from his father, Christopher Columbus Miller. Within a decade it became a hotel, the Glenwood Inn, which flourished with the coming of the railroads. Then in 1902 Frank Miller set

> Arthur B. Benton, Myron Hunt, and G. Stanley Wilson · 1902–44
> Riverside, California

out, with other businessmen, to greatly enlarge the inn. At an estimated cost of $250,000, he built a U-shaped, 275-room hotel that he eventually filled with treasures collected from his trips to the East Coast, Central America, Europe, and Asia.

Zona Gale, author of *Frank Miller of Mission Inn* (1938), notes that Henry E. Huntington, nephew of the Union Pacific Railway's Collis P. Huntington and himself the streetcar king of Los Angeles, contributed $75,000, almost a third of the cost, to build the hotel. In 1902 a virtual war was being fought between competing railroads in this area—the Santa Fe, the Southern (later Union) Pacific, and the smaller San Pedro, Los Angeles, and Salt Lake Railway. The two major lines actually had roadbeds and tracks alongside each other in Riverside and in the 1920s built stations not far from the hotel; a pergola, no longer in existence, connected the stations to the inn.

Railroads almost always built their new stations in the Mission Revival style, probably to capitalize on the romantic notion, promoted by Helen Hunt Jackson's *Ramona* (1884), of California as a paradise before the invasion of the railroads. It followed that a new hotel dependent on the railroads be in the style that the rail barons decreed. Miller chose Arthur B. Benton (1858–1927), a Los Angeles architect who was, with Charles Fletcher Lummis, a founding member of the California Landmarks Club, formed in 1894 to preserve what was left of the Spanish missions.

❧ Above. A 1943 fire destroyed the inn's original chimes tower, which was rebuilt to the designs of G. Stanley Wilson the following year. It was a little taller than the original so that a carillon could be installed.

❧ Left. The west side of The Cloister and the Spanish Wing (1913) at the Mission Inn in Riverside enclose the beautiful Court of the Birds, now used for outdoor dining.

At the time Miller began to expand his inn, the Federal Indian School moved from Perris, a small town fifteen miles away, to the fringe of Riverside. The mission would thus have its Indians. After the inn opened, lace and other handicrafts that Indian children were taught to make at the school were sold in the hotel's gift shop. It all came together in 1909 when Elbert Hubbard, the "Sage of East Aurora," visited and dubbed the inn's impresario "Fra Frank."

In 1913, when Miller decided to add a new wing to the rear of the main building, he asked Myron Hunt (1868–1952) to be his architect. Benton was still practicing, but Hunt's Congregational Church (1913), of which Frank Miller was a member, was under construction just one block from the inn, and its Spanish baroque tower undoubtedly caught the flamboyant innkeeper's eye. Although Hunt was usually opposed to excess, his Spanish Wing is probably the most exuberant architecture his office ever turned out.

In Miller's mind, however, the inn

was not yet complete. On the northwest corner of the block, where some derelict buildings remained, he envisioned commercial buildings and a St. Francis Chapel to house a Mexican altarpiece and Tiffany windows he had purchased in 1920. He chose a local architect, G. Stanley Wilson (1879–1958), and work began in 1930. In addition to the chapel, Wilson gave him a rotunda with circular staircases and a magnificent dome. The complex was now essentially finished.

The Great Depression halted construction, and Miller's death in 1935 seemed to mark the end of a dream. After World War II the inn remained the social center of Riverside, but financial problems and attempts at modernizing the hotel spoiled the ambience that Miller had created. The Craftsman lobby has been lost in applications of paint and colorful rugs. The Stickley and Limbert furniture is gone, as are most of Miller's collections of curios that once amused visitors; some treasures are housed in a small museum at the inn's southwest corner, and more are stored in the basement. Nevertheless the Mission Inn remains, especially on the exterior, a relic of California's instant history and is once again doing a brisk business.

❦ Above. Probably the Mission Inn's greatest treasures are the seven Tiffany glass windows that Frank Miller bought in 1920 when the Madison Square Presbyterian Church (1906, McKim, Mead and White) was destroyed. Shown is a translucent Favrile glass set up on the south side of the chapel; on the other side are opaque iridescent glass windows lighted by electric lights.

❦ Opposite. The St. Francis Chapel (1930), the work of G. Stanley Wilson, was built to house a Mexican baroque altar that Miller purchased on one of his many trips.

❧ Opposite. In 1928 G. Stanley Wilson designed the Mission Inn's Rotunda Wing, which includes a spectacular spiral staircase interwoven with tiers of Spanish arcades.

❧ Above. The corner dome of the Rotunda Wing shows the strong influence of Bertram Goodhue's California Building at the Panama-California Exposition of 1915.

OLD FAITHFUL INN

Robert Reamer · 1903–4
Yellowstone National
Park, Wyoming

For a wilderness experience with none of its discomforts, the Old Faithful Inn is the ultimate Craftsman destination. Before it was built, wealthy tourists, arriving by the Northern Pacific Railway at the north end of Yellowstone National Park, would be transported to the National Hotel in Mammoth Hot Springs. A five-day, round-trip tour costing forty dollars would start there and follow a circuitous route through Yellowstone—designated in 1872 as the world's first national park—making stops at other hotels along the way. The Old Faithful geyser, known for erupting with amazing regularity, was a major attraction, and it quickly became apparent that a hotel was needed nearby for people who wanted to experience this natural phenomenon for longer than the one-hour tour stop.

Harry Child, head of the Yellowstone Park Company, which administered the park for the federal government, commissioned Robert Reamer (1873–1938), an architect for the Great Northern Railway, to design and build this hotel in the Upper Geyser Basin. The choice of a railroad employee is significant, for it signaled the federal government's crucial cooperation with the railroads in developing the West. Before moving to Seattle, Reamer had worked as an architect for the New York, New Haven, and Hartford Railroad. Child called him "the kid"—he was only twenty-nine when hired to design the inn. Given to some youthful exuberance, he was said by Robert Shankland in 1954 to have "sketched the plans while coming shakily out of a monumental submersion in malt, and some authorities claim to be able to read that fact in its unique contours."

Reamer developed a revolutionary conception of what a national park hotel should be. Hotels already stood in Yellowstone Park, but they were similar to resort hotels in the White Mountains and the Catskills—late Queen Anne or Shingle Style. Reamer reasoned that something distinctive was needed to express the golden West. Why not make the Old Faithful Inn a kind of extension of the forest that surrounded it? It would have all the modern conveniences—bathrooms, hot water, good food, and white tablecloths in the dining room—but it would give guests a bosky experience that the eastern hotels could never muster.

The building was conceived to fit into nature rather than contrast with it; thus, Reamer designed a horizontal log base and brown-shingled upper floors. Whether consciously or not, he was following the typical Craftsman precept that a house should never swear at its surroundings. "I built in keeping with the place where it stands," Reamer wrote. "Nobody could improve upon that. To be at discord with the landscape would be almost a crime. To try to improve upon it would be an impertinence."

182

❦ From this vantage point, the six-story inn looks as it did in 1904. Two wings (not visible here), both designed by Robert Reamer, were added in the next decade. Legions of park visitors have watched Old Faithful's powerful volcanic spray from the porches here.

Putting this theory into action, the architect set out on a construction project that would leave modern ecologists writhing in horror. To build what one visitor called "the craftsman's dream realized," he felled a large part of the surrounding forest. Construction began with about forty workers, most of whom had built trestles for the Great Northern. Because the building had to be finished in one year, they were required to labor through Wyoming's harsh winter.

First constructed was the vast fireplace, made of rhyolite rocks from a nearby quarry and marked by four large boulder surrounds with four smaller ones at each corner. The fireplace served as a support for construction of the lobby's seven-story atrium, a great space surrounded by balconies buttressed by log pillars with wooden branches serving as capitals. Railings and newel posts also came directly from the forest; limbs were originally set in place with the bark left on. The final touch was a tree house near the top of the lobby. Beyond this was a rustic staircase that took guests to the roof, where a searchlight had been installed so that they could view Old Faithful's nocturnal eruptions or bears roaming the lawns.

Off in what is now called the Old House were the bedrooms, some large with sets of windows, others tiny with only one window. Walled with rough wood paneling or horizontal pine logs, the rooms were well equipped with washbasins and chamber pots (bathrooms were, as the saying goes, down the hall), steam heat, and electric lights in white candlestick fixtures designed by Reamer.

The architect was called on again in 1913–14 to add east and west wings to the inn and then again in 1927 to extend the porte cochere at the front in the original rustic style. A new government policy had ended the use of local material resources, so the new wings were less woodsy than the old ones but had more modern amenities.

The Old Faithful Inn was essentially finished on schedule. Well-heeled guests could spend untroubled days—as many as they liked—touring geysers in the national park and then come back to the inn, where civilization was marvelously graced by nature. They could have dinner in a forest of transformed pines. The once frightening wilderness had at last been tamed.

❰ Opposite. The log corner detail accents the inn's rusticity. Reamer's use of natural materials to capture the park's natural beauty no doubt inspired the National Park Service some years later to develop its own distinctive style of "parkitecture."

❰ Right. Reamer designed an elevated passageway to connect the Old Faithful Inn's two wings to the Old House. Today the hotel offers some five hundred guest rooms.

❦ Opposite. Balconies of burled lodgepole pine ringing the 92-foot-tall atrium pick up the inn's forest motif. Balustrades seem to have been made from a nest of fallen branches, while posts branch into peculiarly American capitals that neither the Greeks nor the Romans would have recognized.

❦ Above. The inn's fireplace, despite damage from a 1959 earthquake, remains the central feature in a wildly spirited interior forest. On the chimney's north face Robert Reamer placed an iron clock of his own design, produced by local workers.

‍ Above. A lavish $28,000 was spent for the
Old Faithful Inn's furnishings, which ran to
Indian rugs, hickory rocking chairs, and
leather-topped tables—some of them relatively dainty contrasts to the overpowering
force of nature expressed in the hotel.

‍ Right. The stairway and the catwalk lead
to the roof, where in the inn's early days a
searchlight made it possible for guests to see
the bears prowling the lawns at night.

GRAND CANYON NATIONAL PARK

At the south rim of the Grand Canyon, just a few yards from the front door of the El Tovar Hotel (1905, Charles Whittlesey), stands a structure that looks like an ancient pueblo. Known as the Hopi House (1905), it was designed by Mary Colter (1869–1958), an architect from the Midwest who became an authority on American Indian art and lore. Her expertise attracted the attention of the administrators of the Harvey House restaurants, which worked in tandem with the Santa Fe Railway to provide visitor centers for the line's passenger stations. Fred Harvey had first hired Colter to decorate and organize displays in the company's Indian Building (1902) at the Alvarado Hotel in Albuquerque, New Mexico. This com-

Mary Elizabeth Jane Colter
1905-31, Grand Canyon
National Park, Arizona

mission at the Grand Canyon launched her on a career of designing almost entirely for Harvey and the Santa Fe, an association that lasted until 1949.

Colter's interest in American Indians began early in her life. Born in Pittsburgh, she was eleven years old when her family moved to St. Paul, Minnesota, not far from a resident Sioux Indian population. A relative's gift to her family of a number of Sioux items, among them some drawings that Colter prized to the end of her life, set her to collecting Indian art, particularly jewelry, and by the 1890s she had an impressive collection.

The fascination with American Indians was national, largely the result of the success of Helen Hunt Jackson's *Ramona* (1884). Colter's enthusiasm too could undoubtedly be traced to that book, even though she never seems to have mentioned it. In 1903 George Dorsey's *Indians of the Southwest* was published, providing much information about Native Americans to the general public. Shops selling Navajo and Hopi pottery, baskets, and rugs opened across the United States.

❦ Looking as if pueblo residents had just departed, Colter's Hopi House (1905) was her first complete building. Inside, it was equally authentic, with "mud" floors (cement), "adobe" walls (plaster), and "vigas" (log beams). It served as an entertainment center, a museum, and a salesroom for native crafts.

❦ Left. For the Watchtower at Desert View (1931), built along the eastern end of the Grand Canyon's south rim, Colter reached back to ancient Indian ruins to capture the stunning Painted Desert scenery. The building was not a copy, she insisted, but a "recreation," because "various ruins contributed characteristic features." The tall tower allowed Colter to entice sightseers up high for panoramic views. With its meticulously composed local stonework, it looks ancient, but a steel frame undergirds it. Adjacent to the tower is an above-ground kiva.

❦ Above. Inside the tower awaits a veritable museum of southwestern Indian art on three levels. The Hopi painter Fred Kabotie painted intricate murals depicting native myths. The most famous is this depiction of the Hopi snake legend, its four quadrants recording the perennial quest for rain in the desert.

❮ Opposite. In 1935–36 the Harvey Company replaced the old Bright Angel Hotel with a new lodge and surrounding rustic cabins, all designed by Mary Colter. Beneath a forest of posts and beams, a fireplace in the lobby displays immense Kaibab limestone boulders beneath an outspread thunderbird.

❮ Right. Another Bright Angel Lodge fireplace in the lodge's former lounge replicates the Grand Canyon's geological strata in its own layers of stone.

Representing a link with the handwork of the past, Indian crafts—much like the medieval trades that William Morris glorified—became closely associated with the Arts and Crafts movement in America. In descriptions of Craftsman houses, for example, writers often mentioned how compatible Navajo rugs were with the straight lines of Craftsman (at the time always called Mission) furniture. A writer for *Architect and Engineer* observed of one room in 1906, not without condescension, that "the baskets and other paraphernalia are reminders that the original inhabitants of the United States are fitted for other accomplishments than the use of the scalping knife and the chase."

Colter's appreciation of Indian handcrafts was closely allied to her interest in the Arts and Crafts movement. In St. Paul she had been active in the Art Worker's Guild, founded in 1902. In 1909 she gave a lecture entitled "The Red Craftsman," a discourse on Indian pottery and baskets, to St. Paul's New Century Club, using stereopticon images to back up her remarks. A local newspaper praised her work in teaching freehand and mechanical drawing: "Miss M.E.J. Colter has contributed very definitely through her work in the Mechanic Arts High School to the Art and Craft development of the city."

Colter had studied art in San Francisco at the California School of Design, headed by Arthur Mathews, who, with his wife, Lucia, was a leader of the city's Arts and Crafts movement. It was not until she was employed in 1905 to design Hopi House, however, that she became an architect, although her work for an architect in San Francisco had given her the fundamentals. She decided to model the structure in Grand Canyon Village on Hopi pueblos she had seen at Oraibi, an Anasazi settlement in northeastern Arizona. Colter also determined to use similar materials—limestone, sandstone, and peeled logs—and even designed ladders to lean against the walls of roof terraces. (Her quest for authenticity was stretched when she had to use steel rails from the Santa Fe Railway to span large spaces.) Several Hopi families were brought in to live on the upper floors; Nampeyo, a famous Hopi potter, was imported, as were her husband and sons to perform dances for visitors.

Colter's other buildings at Grand Canyon National Park, such as Hermit's Rest (1914) and Lookout Studio (1914), were more like caves or extensions of the powerful terrain than Pueblo Revival dwellings. But a later building on the canyon's rim, the Watchtower at Desert View (1931), was inspired by the Round Tower at the Cliff Palace in Mesa Verde National Park and filled with Indian lore. The challenge here, she wrote, "was to design a building that would become a part of its surroundings;—one that would create no discordant note against the time eroded walls of this promontory." Colter wanted something that would look like a "prehistoric building," that would "blend with the eroded stone cliffs of the Canyon walls themselves." There could be no better statement of the Arts and Crafts desire to build with nature.

197

❦ While Mary Colter's other Grand Canyon structures fit into their cultural and historical landscapes, her Lookout Studio (1914) blends almost seamlessly into the canyon's native limestone itself. The observation station rises respectfully from the promontory as if it were merely a knobby outcropping, an intrinsic part of nature.

❦ Above. Like other romantic architects of the period, Mary Colter spun stories about her buildings to guide their design. At Hermit's Rest (1914) the tale was that of a reclusive prospector who gathered together found materials for a rude shelter. Cascading boulders and plain logs tell the story.

❦ Right. A waystation for weary travelers, Hermit's Rest beckoned visitors indoors with an oversized cave of a fireplace, elevated and set apart like so many Arts and Crafts inglenooks. The stones were purposefully darkened to lend it instant age.

VAN BRIGGLE POTTERY

People who speak (and write) on pottery may well represent the largest cohort of Craftsman devotees. Certainly an admiration for pots was a strong factor in the 1960s revival of appreciation for handcrafted products made in the early twentieth century. The ceramics of Rookwood, Grueby, Roseville, and other potters became collectors' items no matter their quality. Prices soared and have continued to do so.

One early potter whose fame has been rekindled is Artus Van Briggle (1869–1904), who entered the Cincinnati Academy of Art at the age of seventeen. Like many young people in this midwestern haven of the Arts and Crafts, he then found a job at the renowned Rookwood Pottery. Its owner, Maria Longworth Storer, recognized his artistic promise and sent him to Paris to study at the Julian School of Art. There he excelled in drawing and painting but was attracted to ceramics, particularly after a display of fourteenth-century Ming Dynasty pottery at the Sevres Porcelain Factory caught his eye. He was taken with the soft, luminous matte glazes of the Chinese ceramics and determined to discover the process by which these "dead" glazes were achieved.

When he returned to the Rookwood Pottery, Van Briggle began experimenting with glazes on a small gas kiln that Storer had given him, working until he discovered the secret of the matte finish and mastered the wavy lines of Art Nouveau. One of his vases in this style, named "Lorelei" (see page 21), was entered in the Paris Exhibition of 1900. Another design, shown in the exhibition the next year, was bought by the Louvre for three thousand dollars. His career as a ceramist was assured.

Nicolas Van den Arend · 1907–8
Colorado Springs, Colorado

❰ Opposite. The plaque in the Van Briggle Pottery's western gable has the entwined A's for Artus and Anne that became the company's logo. The shuttered window on top is Dutch, while the first-floor window cast in terra cotta looks Richardsonian.

❰ Below. The factory's Dutch allusions became simply a backdrop for Anne's dazzling tiles, interposed in unexpected places—chimney caps, for example—and with a flamboyance that even Henry Mercer could not match. Gables, fireplaces, walls, and floors are covered with tiles, a great many in flower motifs, some of them anticipating Art Deco.

But just as he was tasting success, Van Briggle discovered that he had tuberculosis. In 1899 he packed some of his gear and set out for Colorado Springs, where his health so improved that he was able to establish his own pottery. The following year Anne Gregory, a schoolteacher whom he had met and courted in Paris, joined him. They were married in 1902, and Anne gradually became so involved in the design and making of ceramics that the couple began stamping the bottom of their pots with a monogram of joined A's.

Soon after the company started to win awards, Van Briggle's tuberculosis returned. He died in 1904, having seen only four years of active production. Anne, with experience in administration as well as pottery making, took over the business. As a memorial to her husband, she decided to build a state-of-the-art factory that was also a work of art. She hired a local architect, Nicolas Van den Arend (1870–1940), to design a building reflecting Van Briggle's Dutch descent. The result was a structure that echoed the form of a Dutch farmhouse, its exterior brickwork laid in Flemish bond.

As functional as the building was, its salient features were the tile ornaments that Anne conceived of and then carried out with the help of one of her students, Emma Kincaid McCormick. It was as if Van Briggle's death had spurred her into unexpected creativity. Suddenly she was producing tiles with his matte glaze but in patterns he never dreamed of. Actually Van Briggle had never produced tiles. Now, inspired by his essays into Art Nouveau pottery, Anne derived her ornament from what she called "Colorado colors"—gray, brown, green, lavender—and from Colorado wildflowers. And, as one of her admirers has written, she executed them in three types: "machine-pressed, hand-glazed, single color tiles; hand-pressed and decorated polychrome tiles, in which the glaze is applied onto pressed designs that serve as troughs to contain the different pigments; and the most dramatic of the three—the molded, hand colored three-dimensional tiles."

In 1910 Anne changed the name of the company to Van Briggle Pottery and Tile Company to note its expansion into a new medium. As the factory's tile output increased, even after she remarried in 1912 and spent less time on production, her decorative patterns multiplied; one scholar has counted at least five hundred tile designs that were produced while Anne managed the company. A favorite was a group of tiles that depicted Monument Valley, where the Van Briggle factory was built, with Pike's Peak in the background.

The original factory is well maintained by Colorado College as the headquarters of its maintenance plant. The exterior is easily visible, but the building, which included a showroom and an office, is rarely open. More accessible is the former YMCA building (1912–13) at 130 West Kiowa Street, also designed by Van den Arend. Decorated with Van Briggle tiles outside and in the foyer, it also displays Van Briggle fireplaces on several floors. Another reasonably accessible site is the residence of Arthur Sharp, built about 1910, now the Red Cross headquarters. But the greatest installations of Van Briggle fireplaces in Colorado Springs are in homes in its North End and the Broadmoor Hotel area, most rarely open to the public. The company continues to make pottery today in a new location.

❦ The factory's north end housed the kilns, as evidenced by its two large chimneys. A plaque illustrating a kiln is purely for decoration, while a tiled sign advertises the company.

❆ Above and opposite. The showroom was not large, but it had room for an inglenook. These tiles are among the first that Anne Van Briggle designed as a memorial to her husband, marking her entrance into what was for her a totally new branch of ceramics.

❆ Left. The use of tile in the Van Briggle office is more conservative than in the showroom, although the niche above the mantel recalls the three-dimensional but slightly later work of Henry Mercer.

❆ Right. The pavement of the showroom floor illustrates a variation of the conjoined A's that became the pottery's logo, previously stamped on the base of vases and other Van Briggle wares.

CRAFTSMAN REVIVAL

KUBLY HOUSE

William Morris and Company and the Bauhaus would seem to be the antithesis of each other—the Craftsman celebrating the sanctity of individual workmanship and disdaining the machine, the modernist worshiping the machine's clean lines and scorning ornament and historic styles. The distinction between the two seems clear and for the most part true. Yet Sir Nicholas Pevsner, in *Pioneers of Modern Design: From William Morris to Walter Gropius* (1936), made the case that the Craftsman point of view is the basis for modernism, that Gropius's Bauhaus is in the tradition of Morris. Although Pevsner did not like Morris's medievalizing and what he thought was his anti-machine bias, he appreciated the great craftsman's plea for simplicity and his championing of the dignity of crafts.

Craig Ellwood · 1965
Pasadena, California

Craig Ellwood (1922–92), the architect of the Kubly House, was a fervent advocate of this progressive view of architectural history—that Morris began the trend toward a machine aesthetic that ends with modern architecture. At about the time the house was being constructed, following a lecture on modernism at Occidental College, he was asked, "But Mr. Ellwood, what comes after modern architecture?" Ellwood's answer was swift: "There will only be architecture!"

❦ Right. Like other young architects in the 1960s, Craig Ellwood was attracted to Mies van der Rohe's "Less is more" doctrine, an inspiration obvious in the Kubly House's exterior. Using the material that fits so well into California's architectural tradition, it could be Mies's Farnsworth House (1951), only in wood.

208

❦ Below. Talking about Los Angeles in the 1950s, Ellwood called it "eager for experiment. The feeling that, finally, we were going to get the chance to create a truly honest architecture was like wine in the air," he told Leon Whiteson in an interview published by the *Los Angeles Times* in 1989. At the Kubly House he stripped a house to its bare essentials.

◖ Opposite. Except for the dark wood frame, which was shocking when the house was new, it is difficult to believe that the Kubly House is four decades old. Walls were forsaken in favor of windows that erase the border between inside and out. Although modernist, the design harkens back to Frank Lloyd Wright's belief that walls should be screens, not barriers.

◖ Below. Modern architects built their essays in "Less is more" architecture and then hired landscape architects to screen them from public view. In this case the landscape architect was Craig Ellwood, and he succeeded in bringing nature right into the bedroom while offering a sense of privacy.

Ellwood was born in Clarendon, Texas, but his family soon moved to Los Angeles, victims of the Great Depression. After serving in the U.S. Army Air Force during World War II, he returned to Los Angeles and, with considerable personal flair (he wanted to be a movie star), he dropped his original name, John Burke. He became Craig Ellwood, a name he made up by joining two names taken from a commercial business and doubling the "L's." He called himself "a constructed persona," an intriguing comment on his denial of the past—a trait of the modernist movement.

Ellwood got a job as a cost estimator with the construction firm Lamport Cofer and Salzman, which was building houses by the modernists Harwell Hamilton Harris, Charles Eames, Raphael Soriano, A. Quincy Jones, and Richard Neutra. At the same time he was also taking extension courses in engineering at UCLA. His work and his studies led to his ability to see past conventional building, or as he explained it: "I studied structural engineering, not architecture. And I spent two years in the construction field before I designed. Being a cost estimator in construction, it was easy to see the many ways architects unnecessarily added to construction costs. I was not tied to traditional methods, materials and detailing taught in architectural schools. Therefore I had no inhibitions about experimenting."

Ellwood had no real training in architecture, but in the 1950s and 1960s he was the best-published architect west of Chicago. His mentor was Ludwig Mies van der Rohe (1886–1969), the former director of the Bauhaus in Germany who had become the dean of the architecture school at the Illinois Institute of Technology. "He was the architect I wanted to be," Ellwood once commented, and no one excelled him in designing in the master's cool, classical modern spirit, not even Philip Johnson (b. 1906), whose 1949 glass house in New Canaan, Connecticut, is now so famous. In 1951 John Entenza, editor of *Arts and Architecture* magazine, asked Ellwood to design number 16 in his series of Case Study Houses—a design so successful that Entenza commissioned him to do two more.

❦ Above. The fireplace, a sine qua non of Craftsman living rooms, is here presented against a stark white wall. One is reminded of the hearth in the Freeman dining room (page 78).

❦ Left. Everything in the Kubly House—the placement of the picture, the tubular Breuer chairs, even the view into the kitchen—seems carefully edited in the modern tradition.

In the early 1960s Donald Kubly, president of the Art Center College of Design in Pasadena, purchased a lot in the city's Arroyo Seco area with the idea of building a house that would reflect his and his wife's progressive spirit. Ellwood, then at the height of his fame, was an obvious choice as architect. The Kublys determined that they could afford a house costing about $37,500, but when Ellwood proposed that it be framed in steel, his favorite building material, the estimated cost ran about $50,000 over their budget. Asked to reconsider the building's structure, Ellwood finally suggested wood, although he was a bit edgy about this substitution: "The mistake that most architects make in using steel is to treat it as wood," he observed. "Maybe we are guilty in reversing this; eccentric loading columns are much easier with steel."

213

But the result is that this 2,150-square-foot house fits into its bosky site almost as if Ellwood were trying to follow the Craftsman aesthetic of the woodsy houses built by earlier neighbors in the Arroyo Seco. The Kublys' mundane requirement of economy provides an amusing proof of Nicholas Pevsner's thesis that William Morris's desire for simplicity was the beginning of the modern movement in architecture. The Kubly House marks its end.

But not quite: In the 1970s, when Kubly's college built its new campus on a hill not far from the house, Ellwood was given the commission to construct a bridge that also served as a classroom and administration building. He produced another landmark in the International Style, but history had passed him by. New architectural modes from brutalism to postmodernism to neoexpressionism had appeared, all contradicting the machine aesthetic. Ellwood's earlier prophesy did not pan out. "My architecture was rigid and I've always been a romantic at heart," he wrote in 1978, adding that architecture "wasn't exciting anymore." He stopped designing and went to Italy.

But to return to the lecture question: Why should anything have to lead anywhere historically? Why not just say that William Morris spoke for a certain element of society in his time and that Craig Ellwood did likewise?

KAPPE HOUSE

Ray Kappe · 1965–68
Pacific Palisades,
California

As it moved from Europe to the United States, the International Style underwent a sea change. The style that had denied personal expression and followed the exclusionist "Less is more" doctrine was softened to such a degree that pure examples in America—Philip Johnson's Glass House (1949), Mies van der Rohe's Farnsworth House (1951), Craig Ellwood's Kubly House (1965)—are rare. Why the change?

There are several reasons, the primary one being that it is difficult to separate personality from art. An informed eye can easily detect differences in style between Le Corbusier (1887–1965), Walter Gropius (1883–1969), and Ludwig Mies van der Rohe (1886–1969), the principal champions of an architecture divorced from romanticism and its cult of individuality. Their buildings may be difficult to distinguish from those of their best students, but these fathers of modernist architecture speak for themselves, whatever their attempt to follow a universal thesis. Selflessness may be the attitude of saints but not architects—at least not American architects.

❦ Right. Just as the entire house is surrounded by woods, so is the entrance, in this case milled wood. Here at the front of the Kappe House nature and art are intermingled.

❦ Below. The corner of the master bedroom plays verticals and horizontals—along with wood, glass, and plaster—against each other. A lot is going on here, in a quiet way.

Even European modernists who came to the United States with their spartan aesthetic were at the mercy of America's relaxed ambience. Richard Neutra (1892–1970), trained in Vienna to believe that "ornament is crime," expressed himself so strongly in his Lovell House (1929)—without abdicating his convictions—that he was scolded for his expressionism by Philip Johnson and Henry Russell-Hitchcock in their catalogue for the 1932 International Style show at the Museum of Modern Art. Neutra's friend R. M. Schindler (1887–1953), also a product of Viennese modernism, was excluded from the exhibition because he seemed too close to Frank Lloyd Wright in his personal expression and style (Wright was also excluded).

Certainly Wright (1867–1959) is a significant figure in the story of America's "soft modernism." Both Schindler, who worked for him, and Neutra admired his work, but others not so close to Wright also held him in reverence, although, like Neutra and Schindler, they rarely imitated him in any way. Wright, on the other hand, had nothing but contempt for the modernist movement. However, as the architectural historian Vincent Scully has shown, Wright took Neutra's modernist Lovell House and romanticized it. The result was Fallingwater (1935), probably Wright's most popular work.

Unlike the International Style, soft modernism does not get its kicks from its contrast with nature; rather, it welcomes nature as another player in the game. Surely that is the attitude of Ray Kappe, who designs houses of glass and steel—and wood—with large expanses of windows that let nature in. Kappe (b. 1927) was born in Minneapolis but later moved with his family to Los Angeles, where he attended a junior high school designed by Neutra. He entered the University of California at Berkeley just as its architecture school was making a transition from Beaux-Arts to Bauhaus teaching. After graduation in 1951, Kappe worked independently, designing multiple-unit and commercial projects in addition to forty residences before 1968, when the partnership Kahn Kappe Lotery Boccato was formed. Equally important was his role as educator. In 1969 he was chosen as the founding chairman of the new architecture school at California State Polytechnic University in Pomona, and three years later he helped establish the Southern California School of Architecture, one of the most imaginative programs in the country. His wife, Shelly Kappe, the school's cofounder, also taught architectural history there. Both retired in 1987.

❨ Above. In the library wood dominates, with walls continuing the same material as the floors for a seamless unity. Built-in bookcases and furniture carry out the Craftsman ideal of simplicity. The mattress on the floor is a staple of entertaining in southern California.

❨ Opposite. A view from the dining room into the living room also includes Ray Kappe's studio on the lower floor. Above it is the library. The wood beams were used to direct the interior prospect out to nature.

❧ Opposite. The living room's design confuses the eye as to what is wall and what is space, what is indoors and what is outdoors. The Kappe residence is a Craftsman tree house in just about every respect.

❧ Below. Is this passageway inside or outside? The beam between the hall and the living room is all that defines space, a design tactic borrowed from Frank Lloyd Wright's Prairie style. The tiles marking the walkway and the brick wall further blur the distinction between inside and outside.

Their own house is located in Rustic Canyon, a former arboretum that gets its moisture from the fogs that roll in from the nearby Pacific Ocean and from underground springs, a combination that has created one of Los Angeles's miniclimates, where everything grows. The site posed problems: because of the numerous springs, the hillside was not stable. To handle vertical loads and seismic features, Kappe designed six concrete towers that support the 4,000-square-foot structure. Ties were made with exposed laminated beams that reflect the natural contours of the site. The Kappe House became the prototype for several other houses in Rustic Canyon and other similar hillsides.

As with the earlier Bay Area houses designed by Louis Christian Mullgardt, the approach to the Kappe House is part of the visual experience. Slab concrete steps lead to a zigzag path, which in turn leads across a wooden bridge and up to the front door. The entrance offers a choice of going downstairs to Kappe's studio or upstairs to the living room, dining room, and kitchen, all one large space; at the northeast and southwest ends are the bedrooms. This space is lighted by skylights over the tower units, by clerestory windows, and by large panels of glass that give views of the wooded surroundings.

The liberal use of exposed wooden beams throughout the house is just another way of relating the house to nature. It is unquestionably a modernist structure, but the Craftsman ideal is achieved, whether intended or not. Indeed, the Kappe House points to another path for contemporary architecture.

SKYROSE CHAPEL

When Frank Lloyd Wright (1867–1959) died, some of his eulogists pointed out that although he had trained many students at the Taliesin Fellowship, these students had rarely amounted to anything. That was not quite true. Herb Greene, John Lautner, and Wright's own son Lloyd designed fine buildings to demonstrate their talent and independence. But Fay Jones, associated with Wright at Taliesin for a short time, is the greatest exception to the rule.

Jones (b. 1921) was born in Pine Bluff, Arkansas, in 1921 and grew up in El Dorado, a prosperous town. According to Robert Adams Ivy Jr. in *Fay Jones* (1992), he was inspired to become an architect in 1938 while watching a *Popular Science* film on Wright's Johnson Wax headquarters (1936–42) in Racine, Wisconsin.

E. Fay Jones · 1998
Rose Hills Memorial Park
Whittier, California

Years later Jones remembered that "the film showed Pyrex glass partitions, curving brick walls, light pouring in. It felt like being thrown two centuries ahead in time."

From then on Wright exerted a major influence on Jones. After a short stint in the school of engineering at the University of Arkansas, followed by service as a navy pilot during World War II, Jones entered the new architecture program at Oklahoma A&M and was graduated in its first class in 1950. There he was taught Bauhaus functionalism and subjected to its distaste for historic styles.

But Jones was not taken in by Bauhaus dogma. His interest in Wright's architecture, so different from that of the Bauhaus, took him to Taliesin in 1953. For a short time there he worked as a draftsman. Jones's association with Wright was of fundamental importance in developing his principles of design, particularly for his domestic architecture; there Wright's influence is easily recognized in both details and the manipulation of space.

❡ Right. Fay Jones's outside-in interpretation of the Gothic church brings the flying buttresses inside, where they pull the eye skyward. The sanctuary, one of SkyRose Chapel's three levels, encloses a custom-built pipe organ with 3,937 pipes from four inches to thirty-two feet high.

❡ Below. The architect loves massive roofs that broadcast the Arts and Crafts ideal of shelter. Pitched at forty-five degrees, the chapel's rises to an impressive ninety feet at its peak.

❆ Above. A detail near the east entrance of SkyRose Chapel is a distant relative of Wright's design vocabulary, reminiscent of stylized feathers he etched into his art glass windows.

❆ Left. A pergola—a favored Craftsman technique for uniting outdoors and in—extends the building into the garden. Shadows cast their own built-in ornament on the walkway.

Jones's handful of chapels, for which he is best known, are another matter. Every ecclesiastical building he has designed shows the direct influence of Gothic architecture. As with William Morris, the source of Jones's medievalism is the writings of John Ruskin, especially the chapter "The Nature of Gothic" in *The Stones of Venice* (1852). It was Ruskin, after all, who converted his readers to the notion that Gothic is the religious model. Ruskin's ideas affect us today and stimulate our enjoyment of Fay Jones's churches.

His first was Thorncrown Chapel (1980), a tiny and much-heralded gem in Eureka Springs, Arkansas. By the time he came to design SkyRose Chapel in Whittier, California, he had honed his skills on six perfect little chapels in the woods. Although Jones's churches are usually set into groves of trees, becoming a part of the forest, this hilltop site on ten acres is surrounded by gardens and terraces as well as a small grove of oak, sycamore, jacaranda, and pepper trees. The chapel site in turn rests on what, at 1,400 acres, is considered the largest cemetery in the world in one location—whose views of the greater Los Angeles area provide an incomparable final resting place.

Jones freely admits his derivation of designs from Gothic churches, but he points out that he has actually turned Gothic construction outside in. He employs what he calls an "operative opposite" interpretation, rejecting exterior flying buttresses and instead making structural forces into part of the interior experience. Working with his associate Maurice Jennings, Jones here combined fir and Oregon redwood with canyon stone and glass to create his largest chapel.

Both the forest of arches and the treatment of light at SkyRose Chapel exhibit Jones's "operative opposite" principle. A 105-foot-long skylight tracing the roof's peak throws its beams against the wooden struts, giving the effect of dappling—and contradicting the Gothic attitude toward light, which was to collect it in stained glass windows and darken the interiors. Jones's churches instead are full of magical light.

He remains generous in his praise of other architects, among them Charles and Henry Greene, Bernard Maybeck, and Harwell Hamilton Harris. He acknowledges a debt to Bruce Goff (1904–82), whose work he knew when he taught at the University of Oklahoma. But one senses the fact that these people were sources of inspiration rather than, except for Wright, influences.

When the master visited Jones's own home in 1958, he surveyed the living room and said approvingly, "Fay, I am going to have to give you a certificate." Wright himself recognized a kindred spirit in Fay Jones.

❰ Opposite. Fay Jones's SkyRose Chapel shares the Craftsman emphasis on structure. Plate glass windows of the chapel, which serves weddings, funerals, and musical performances, look out on gardens. A huge west window behind the pulpit frames a magnificent view of the San Gabriel valley.

❰ Below left. Light filtered through the ceiling struts in the nave creates a dappled effect, like sunlight dancing around the leaves of trees surrounding a chapel in the woods.

❰ Below right. The view from the balcony to the ceiling opens up an explosion of forms.

DISNEY'S GRAND
CALIFORNIAN HOTEL

William Morris and Gustav Stickley and all their fellow proponents of the true and simple life should be pleased that the twentieth century ended up being framed by the Arts and Crafts movement: first manifested just as the century was dawning, the Craftsman aesthetic reawakened in the 1960s and shows no sign of winding down even today, a century later. Considering the long and extensive exposure of Arts and Crafts architecture to the public, its revival was not immediate. This may be because it is so difficult to reproduce the spirit of architectural styles without plagiarizing them. But it is clear that we are now experiencing a Craftsman revival. Bungalows are back, and new Craftsman-style homes are being built all over the country. Even in the East Craftsman look-alikes are beginning to intrude into the residential territory long staked out by colonial clones. And offices and restaurants—even hotels—are being outfitted in the Greene and Greene mode.

Peter Dominick, Urban Design Group
Richard Brayton and Walt Disney Imagineering,
Interior Design · 2001
Disneyland, Anaheim, California

Disney's Grand Californian Hotel, with 750 rooms and 1,300 parking spaces, is a special case. It is adjacent to the original Disneyland Park in Anaheim and is an integral part of a new theme park, Disney's California Adventure, making the hotel one of a trio of attractions. After deciding on California's heritage, from the gold rush to Hollywood, as the focus of the new park, hotel planners at Walt Disney Imagineering considered a range of architectural styles associated with the state. They rejected Mission and modern in favor of Arts and Crafts, both because the style seemed to fill a void and because it would allow them to try their hand at emulating the craftsmen of a century ago.

❆ Left. Sinuous entrance gates to the new Disney's Grand Californian Hotel at Disneyland Resort, simulating a California redwood forest, were fashioned by Tim Burrows of Missouri to ease the transition from the surrounding Downtown Disney esplanade. There the architecture, fixtures, and colors are designed in a contrasting Art Deco style.

❆ Below. Despite its commercial scale, the hotel's exterior quickly conveys key signatures of the Craftsman style: wide, sweeping roofs; projecting beams; exaggerated braces and other assertive timberwork; and colors that blend with nature.

On the exterior Disney's Grand Californian looks like a national park hotel—say, the Old Faithful Inn (1903–4) at Yellowstone. But the interior is where the action is. Recognizable details from various Craftsman buildings are everywhere. The reception hall, for example, is an interpretation of the interior of the tiny Swedenborgian Church (1894) by A. C. Schweinfurth (1864–1900) in San Francisco.

Then one enters the Great Hall—and great it is! Here the architects, led by Peter Dominick of the Urban Design Group, faced the challenge of how to construct and design a living room (lobby) on an immense scale when the typical Craftsman interior was residential and therefore intimate. Solution: Keeping in mind that the Craftsman house was almost always set in a garden, think of increasing the proportions of a garden to those of a forest. The stems of flowers become the limbs of trees that translate into beams in the Great Hall's ceiling. This change in scale obviously demands the enlargement of details taken from the vocabulary of Greene and Greene, Maybeck, and Wright. One thing follows another.

A major concern of the interior designers, led by Richard Brayton and the Walt Disney Imagineering staff, was to impart a "handmade" quality to everything from furniture to lamps, art tiles and pottery, stained glass, metalware, paintings, wood carvings, paintings, and tapestries. Some of the artifacts are antiques from the first Arts and Crafts period, such as a case containing articles made by Elbert Hubbard's Roycrofters, but other displays were made more recently by artisans such as modern Roycrofters working today in East Aurora, New York. (The early Roycroft can be distinguished from the new by the stamp: a double R in place of the old, a single R.) Most of the objects, however, were created by Disney cast members. The Tiffany-style lamps were locally made, although using equipment that once was the property of Tiffany and Company. Plein-air paintings were inspired by such vintage artists as Benjamin Brown, Arthur Mathews, Franz Bischoff, Maurice Braun, Marion Cavanaugh Wachtel, and other Californians. Woodblock prints recall the best of Gustave Baumann's work. Bird sculptures that strongly resemble the designs of the English Martin brothers are, one learns, not the real thing.

229

❰ Left. The reception area of Disney's Grand Californian is modeled on the interior of A. C. Schweinfurth's Church of the New Jerusalem (1895) in San Francisco but is much larger.

❰ Below. One suite at the hotel resurrects the work of the California architects Charles and Henry Greene. New furniture for it was designed by Thomas Strangeland.

❦ Above. Two suites at Disney's Grand Californian pay homage to Frank Lloyd Wright. Feathery art glass reminiscent of his best Prairie style work was created by Susan McCracken of Atlanta.

❦ Opposite. In the Hearthstone Lounge, the Vienna Secession branch of the broad Craftsman tree can be seen. Stripes of redwood veneer lend an abstract tone to the room, whose coffee bar carries the carved aphorism "Nature is the source of all artistic expression."

In the Storytellers Cafe is a 1927 tile mural by the Gladding McBean Company for a Robin Hood Room in the Wilmington, California, public library. The Napa Rose restaurant, also designed by Dorf Design, features a rose motif inspired by the Glasgow tearooms of Charles Rennie Mackintosh. The California Boardroom, with its barrel-vaulted ceiling and art glass windows, resembles the playroom in Frank Lloyd Wright's own house in Oak Park. Suites of rooms are dedicated to the ideas of Wright and his Prairie School colleagues and also those of Greene and Greene, but the designers do not copy. They interpret these architects' legacy.

Ecological concerns were respected by the designer of the Hearthstone Lounge, who, instead of cutting down a redwood tree to make the paneling, found a tree that had fallen naturally and bought it. Women are acknowledged in paintings and sculptures in a game room that was traditionally for men only. Suddenly one realizes that not only is one being entertained; one is also being educated. A century of Craftsman theory and history is housed here under one large roof.

Right. The hotel's Great Hall reception area wows visitors with the same impressive use of space found in historic Craftsman lodgings such as the Old Faithful Inn. Beams branch overhead in the atrium to create a forest of woodwork, while the open balcony provides plenty of good vantage points. An oversized fireplace of cascading boulders and arboreal motifs anchors one side.

Below. A gatehouse outside the hotel introduces motifs—rustic stonework, exaggerated timberwork, arched openings, and a natural color scheme—that reappear inside Disney's Grand Californian. The little building's hat of intersecting beams and braces is just a hint of the special effects to come.

SOURCES

Introduction *(pages 16–29)*

Page 18: See Richard Hofstadter's *The Age of Reform* (New York: Vintage, 1960) and T. J. Jackson Lears's *No Place of Grace: Antimodernism and the Transformation of American Culture 1880–1920* (New York: Pantheon, 1981), especially pp. 57-96. "It was his instinct. . . .": Fiona MacCarthy, *William Morris: A Life for Our Time* (New York: Knopf, 1995), p. 605.

Page 19: "Apart from a desire to produce beautiful things. . . .": Lears, p. 62. "When he came to build his own house. . . .": MacCarthy, p. 602.

Page 28: See *Bay Area Houses,* edited by Sally Woodbridge (Salt Lake City: Peregrine Smith, 1988).

El Alisal *(pages 32–37)*

Most of the material on Lummis came from his *Journals,* which are in typescript in the libraries of the Southwest Museum and Occidental College. A colorful but disorganized source is Dudley Gordon's *Charles F. Lummis: Crusader in Corduroy* (Los Angeles: Cultural Assets Press, 1972). The best introduction to Lummis's life and works is *Chas. F. Lummis,* edited by Daniela P. Moneta (Los Angeles: Southwest Museum, 1985); this exhibition catalogue contains a list of Lummis's writings and a note on primary sources.

Duncan-Irwin House *(pages 38–49)*

Whereas Greene and Greene were all but unknown half a century ago, publications have poured out since Randell Makinson's chapter on them in Esther McCoy's *Five California Architects* (New York: Praeger, 1960). Since then three major books have been published. Randell Makinson's *Greene and Greene: Architecture as a Fine Art* (Salt Lake City: Peregrine Smith, 1977) was the first and is still valuable. Edward Bosley's *Greene and Greene* (London: Phaidon, 2000) is more recent and has much new material. Bruce Smith and Alexander Vertikoff in their *Greene and Greene: Masterworks* (San Francisco: Chronicle, 1998) tick off major works house by house, with words well chosen and incredibly beautiful photographs. All three books have extensive bibliographies.

Riordan Mansion *(pages 50–57)*

The only biography of Charles F. Whittlesey is the short piece on him in *A Biographical Dictionary of American Architects (Deceased)* (Henry F. and Elsie Rathburn Withey, 1956; reprint, Santa Monica, Calif.: Hennessey and Ingalls, 1970). The best writing on the Riordan House is by Richard Knotts, "Arizona's Arts and Crafts Treasure," *American Bungalow,* no. 31, fall 2001, pp. 16-23.

Fonthill *(pages 58–63)*

Cleota Reed's *Henry Chapman Mercer and the Moravian Tile Works* (Philadelphia: University of Pennsylvania Press, 1987) is an excellent study of the mad genius Henry Mercer.

Craftsman Farms *(pages 64–71)*

As indicated in the text, Jackson Lears's *No Place of Grace* (New York: Pantheon, 1981), pp. 59-96, has a brilliant section on the Arts and Crafts movement. Otherwise, it is best to read *The Craftsman* to get the range of Gustav Stickley's ideas. David Cathers makes a great contribution to the cause in his *Gustav Stickley* (London: Phaidon, 2003) and *Stickley Style: Arts and Crafts Homes in the Craftsman Tradition* (New York: Simon and Schuster, 1999), with elegant photographs by Alexander Vertikoff.

Freeman House *(pages 74–79)*

There is no monograph on Ernest Coxhead, but he is brilliantly interpreted by Richard Longstreth in his *On the Edge of the World: Four Architects in San Francisco at the Turn of the Century* (Cambridge, Mass.: MIT Press, Architectural History Foundation, 1983). I also gained much information from John Beach's "The Bay Area Tradition, 1890-1918" in *Bay Area Houses,* edited by Sally Woodbridge (Salt Lake City: Peregrine Smith, 1988), pp. 24-36.

Hewitt House *(pages 80–85)*

I cannot strongly enough express my debt to Patty Dean's article "It Is Here We Live," *Minnesota History,* no. 57, spring 2001, pp. 244-62. It is based on a description of the house in *The Craftsman,* no. 12, September 1907, pp. 678-82, and describes how over the years the furniture and color schemes have all but disappeared.

Bailey House *(pages 86–93)*

Most writers on Irving Gill have been modernists who give only passing attention to his Craftsman side. In her *Five California Architects* (New York: Praeger, 1960), Esther McCoy covers the Bailey House with two pictures and a caption. Thomas Hines's *Irving Gill and the Architecture of Reform* (New York: Monacelli, 2000) gives it more space but does not say how it was related to "reform." Four excellent photographs and one informative caption is the extent of Bruce Kamerling's treatment of the house in his *Irving J. Gill, Architect* (San Diego: San Diego Historical Society, 1993).

Evans House *(pages 94–99)*

I have tried to indicate in the text my heavy debt to Robert Judson Clark's essay on Mullgardt in *Toward a Simpler Way of Life: the Arts and Crafts Architects of California,* edited by Robert Winter (Berkeley: University of California Press, 1997), pp. 41-50. For the section on planning in Marin County, I am indebted, as in many other places, to Richard Longstreth's *On the Edge of the World* (Cambridge, Mass.: MIT Press, Architectural History Foundation, 1983), in this case pp. 143-50. John Beach's "The Bay Area Tradition, 1890-1918" in *Bay Area Houses,* edited by Sally Woodbridge (Salt Lake City: Peregrine Smith, 1988), pp. 84-86, was also useful.

Caldwell House *(pages 100–103)*

The only writing on Louis B. Easton is by Tim Andersen in the book I edited, *Toward a Simpler Way of Life: The Arts and Crafts Architects of California* (Berkeley: University of California Press, 1997), pp. 149-58.

Gless and Hindry Houses *(pages 104–9)*

A few Heineman papers exist in the Greene and Greene Library at the Huntington Museum in San Marino, Calif. Most of my information has come from Alfred Heineman, who for a few years before his death was my friend. Some details, not registered in this essay, are in an essay I wrote on the Heinemans in *Toward a Simpler Way of Life: The Arts and Crafts Architects of California* (Berkeley: University of California Press, 1997), pp. 137-48.

Roos House *(pages 110–15)*

There are two fine books on Maybeck and his architecture: Sally Woodbridge's *Bernard Maybeck: Visionary Architect* (New York: Abbeville, 1992) and Kenneth Cardwell's *Bernard Maybeck: Artisan, Architect, Artist* (Salt Lake City: Peregrine Smith, 1977). Cardwell was a close friend of Maybeck, and Woodbridge's book includes color photography. Anyone interested in Maybeck should read both books. In his old age Maybeck himself was interviewed many times. The best interview is Gerald Beatty's in the *Berkeley Daily Gazette,* December 26, 1956. It is full of good quotes from Maybeck, including his observation on Frank Lloyd Wright: "Nobody can imitate Wright—I wouldn't, but I couldn't even if I tried. We're both Greeks, Wright and I."

Thomas House *(pages 116–21)*

Sara Holmes Boutelle's beautiful and masterly *Julia Morgan, Architect* (New York: Abbeville, 1988) offers a broad understanding of Morgan. Boutelle does not touch on the Thomas House, but I have been helped by Susan Cerny and our photographer, Alexander Vertikoff.

Dungan House *(pages 122–27)*

There is no monograph on John Hudson Thomas, so the best place to begin a study is in Thomas Gordon Smith's essay in *Toward a Simpler Way of Life: The Arts and Crafts Architects of California*, edited by Robert Winter (Berkeley: University of California Press, 1997). John Beach's "The Bay Area Tradition, 1890–1918" in *Bay Area Houses*, edited by Sally Woodbridge (Salt Lake City: Peregrine Smith, 1988), pp. 90–95, discusses several other Thomas houses. Robert Judson Clark also helped me with this essay.

The Close *(pages 128–33)*

On Baillie Scott the key book is James D. Kornwolf's *M. H. Baillie Scott and the Arts and Crafts Movement: Pioneers of Modern Design* (Baltimore: Johns Hopkins University Press, 1972).

Roycroft Colony *(pages 136–41)*

Freeman Champney's *Art and Glory: The Story of Elbert Hubbard* (Kent, Ohio: Kent State University Press, 1968) is an engaging biography. The Janet Ashbee sequence is taken from an article I wrote, "American Sheaves from C.R.A. and Janet Ashbee," *Journal of the Society of Architectural Historians*, no. 30, December 1971, pp. 317–22. Other information came from *The Oxford Companion to American Literature* (New York: Oxford University Press, 1965).

Rose Valley and Arden *(pages 142–55)*

Most of my knowledge of the Rose Valley community comes from *A Poor Sort of Heaven, A Good Sort of Earth: The Rose Valley Arts and Crafts Experiment*, edited by William Ayres (Chadds Ford, Pa.: Brandywine River Museum, 1983), an exhibition catalogue. Arden is well covered in a short pamphlet, *The Arden Book* (Arden, Del.: Arden Community Planning Committee, 1992; rev. ed., 1999). The work of Will Price is well documented in George E. Thomas's *William L. Price: Arts and Crafts to Modern Design* (New York: Princeton Architectural Press, 2000).

Byrdcliffe *(pages 156–63)*

The source of my material was *The Byrdcliffe Arts and Crafts Colony: Life by Design*, a catalogue for an exhibition in 1984–85 of artifacts from the colony at the Delaware Art Museum in Wilmington; the lead article by Robert Edwards is especially informative.

Bungalow Heaven *(pages 164–71)*

The literature on bungalows is burgeoning, but readers should see my *American Bungalow Style* (New York: Simon and Schuster, 1996), with photographs also by Alexander Vertikoff. About the same time, Paul Duchscherer and Douglas Keister produced *The Bungalow* (New York: Penguin Studio, 1995). There is no solid study of bungalow courts, but they are frequently referred to in *American Bungalow* magazine.

Mission Inn *(pages 174–81)*

The Mission Inn is the primary focus of Karen J. Weitze's "A. B. Benton" in the book I edited, *Toward a Simpler Way of Life: The Arts and Crafts Architects of California* (Berkeley: University of California Press, 1997), pp. 191–200. Esther Klotz's *The Mission Inn: Its History and Artifacts* (Corona, Calif.: UBS Printing Group, 1981; rev. ed. by Alan Curl, 1993) is good on facts. An early source is Zona Gale's *Frank Miller of Mission Inn* (New York: D. Appleton-Century, 1938).

Old Faithful Inn *(pages 182–89)*

For facts in this essay I am indebted to the National Park Service. Several histories of the inn appear on the Old Faithful Inn Web site: www.cr.nps.gov/history/online. All quotes are taken from them. A handy history and description of the inn is Christine Barnes's little *Old Faithful Inn at Yellowstone National Park* (Bend, Ore.: W.W. West, 2001). See also Robert Shankland's *Steve Mather of the National Parks* (New York: Knopf, 1954), p. 117.

Grand Canyon National Park *(pages 190–99)*

Here I have drawn heavily from Arnold Berke's *Mary Colter: Architect of the Southwest* (New York: Princeton Architectural Press, 2002), with photographs by Alexander Vertikoff. It is especially delightful when Berke goes off on tangents such as the history of Harvey House restaurants. His footnotes are rich with relevant books and articles on national parks. The first work on Mary Colter was Virginia L. Grattan's *Mary Colter: Builder upon the Red Earth* (Flagstaff, Ariz.: Northland Press, 1980).

Van Briggle Pottery *(pages 200–205)*

Almost the entire spring 2002 issue of *Kiva* is devoted to the work of Artus and Anne Van Briggle. The most useful article was Roberta McIntyre's "100 Years of Van Briggle Pottery," pp. 16–19, 33-39. Stronger on the architecture of the Van Briggle factory is Sandra Knauf's "The Van Briggle Connection: Carving a Niche in the American Arts and Crafts Revival," *Flash Point*, no. 5, April-June 1992, pp. 1, 8–9, 16. *Flash Point* is the quarterly bulletin of the Tile Heritage Foundation, a valuable source of information on the history of tiles.

Kubly House *(pages 208–13)*

Esther McCoy was the first writer to offer a critical appraisal of Ellwood's work in *Craig Ellwood* (1968; reprint, Santa Monica, Calif.: Hennesey and Ingalls, 1977, California Architecture and Architects, no. 9). More recently Neil Jackson has published *California Modern: The Architecture of Craig Ellwood* (New York: Princeton Architectural Press, 2002), in which he notes the importance of Ellwood's assistants in completing the designs of a man who was not a draftsman. In the same year Alfonso Pérez-Méndez wrote *Craig Ellwood: In the Spirit of the Time* (Barcelona: CG, 2002), an extremely thoughtful book. Also important was Ellwood's much-better-than-average obituary in the *Los Angeles Times* (June 1, 1992) by Burt A. Folkart. I have also had the advantage of hearing the Kublys tell their experiences in building their house. The Pevsner point was inspired by an observation made by Alan Crawford in an unpublished paper: "After Modernism: Towards a Larger Understanding of the Arts and Crafts Movement," 1987.

Kappe House *(pages 214–19)*

Ray Kappe's architecture has been well published in journals, newspapers, and books. Michael Webb's monograph, *Ray Kappe House Design: Themes and Variations* (Mulgrove, Victoria, Australia: Images Publishing Group, 1998), is the best overall view of his work. My essay is based almost entirely on unpublished notes given to me by the architect and also on my personal experience of his house. The concept of "soft modernism" came from my friend Eileen Michels.

SkyRose Chapel *(pages 220–25)*

My single source has been Robert Adams Ivy Jr.'s *Fay Jones* (Washington, D.C.: American Institute of Architects Press, 1992), which contains bibliographical references for Jones and his work. Some basic information is also available on the chapel's Web site: www.rosehills.com.

Grand Californian Hotel *(pages 226–33)*

My essay is based on unpublished material given to me by the Disney Studios. Michelle Gringeri-Brown covered the hotel in her "Disney's Arts and Crafts Showpiece," in *American Bungalow*, no. 32, winter 2001, pp. 48–62, with splendid photographs by Alexander Vertikoff.

VISITING CRAFTSMAN SITES

The following places regularly or occasionally welcome visitors. Please contact the sites to obtain current visitation information.

Public Structures

Riordan Mansion
Riordan Mansion
  State Historic Park
409 Riordan Road
Flagstaff, AZ 86001
928-779-4395
www.pr.state.az.us

Grand Canyon
  National Park
South Rim
Grand Canyon, AZ 86023
520-638-7771, 520-638-7888
www.thecanyon.com

Marston House
San Diego Historical
  Society
3525 Seventh Avenue
San Diego, CA 92103
619-298-3142

Grand Californian Hotel
Disneyland Park
1313 South Harbor
Boulevard
Anaheim, CA 92802
877-700-DISNEY,
  949-494-9499
www.disneyland.com

El Alisal (Lummis House)
200 East Avenue 43
Los Angeles, CA 90031
323-222-0546

Judson Art Glass Studio
200 South Avenue 66
Los Angeles, CA 90042
213-255-0131
www.judsonstudio.com

Gamble House
4 Westmoreland Place
Pasadena, CA 91103
626-793-3334
www.gamblehouse.org

Mission Inn
3649 Mission Inn Avenue
Riverside, CA 92501
909-784-0300
www.missioninn.com

Tor House and
  Hawk Tower
Robinson Jeffers Tor
House Foundation
26304 Ocean View Avenue
Carmel, CA 93923
831-624-1813
www.torhouse.org

Asilomar Conference
  Center
800 Asilomar Boulevard
Pacific Grove, CA 93950
408-372-8016
www.asilomarcenter.com

The Ahwahnee Hotel
Yosemite National Park,
  CA 95389
209-372-1407
www.yosemitepark.com

Van Briggle Art Pottery
(original factory:
  1125 Glen Avenue)
600 South 21st Street
Colorado Springs, CO
80904
719-633-4080

Frank Lloyd Wright
  Home and Studio
951 Chicago Avenue
Oak Park, IL 60302
708-848-1976
www.wrightplus.org

Ragdale (Shaw House)
Ragdale Foundation
1260 North Green Bay
  Road
Lake Forest, IL 60045
847-234-1063
www.ragdale.org

Newcomb Art Gallery
Newcomb College
1229 Broadway
New Orleans, La 70118
504-865-5328
www.newcomb.tulane.edu/
newcpottery.html

Pewabic Pottery
10125 East Jefferson Avenue
Detroit, MI 48214
313-822-0954
www.pewabic.com

Cranbrook
1221 North Woodward
  Avenue
Bloomfield Hills, MI
48303-0801
248-645-3000
www.cranbrook.edu

Craftsman Farms
2352 Route 10 West
Parsippany, NJ 07950
973-540-1165
www.parsippany.net/
craftsmanfarms.html

Stickley Museum
300 Orchard Street
Fayetteville, NY 13066
315-682-5500
www.stickleymuseum.org

Grove Park Inn
290 Macon Avenue
Asheville, NC 28804
800-438-5800
www.groveparkinn.com

Timberline Lodge
Timberline Ski Area
Timberline Lodge,
  OR 97028
503-272-3311
www.timberlinelodge.com

Fonthill and
  Mercer Museum
84 South Pine Street
Doylestown, PA
18901-4999
215-345-0210
www.mercermuseum.org

Moravian Pottery
  and Tile Works
130 Swamp Road
Doylestown, PA 18901
215-345-6722
www.bucksnet.com/
moravian

Old Faithful Inn
Yellowstone National
Park, WY 82190
307-344-7311
www.travelyellowstone.com

Historic Districts

Bungalow Heaven
Washington Boulevard,
  Hill Avenue, Orange
  Grove Boulevard, and
  Lake Avenue
Pasadena, CA
626-585-2172
http://home.earthlink.net/
~bhna

Arden
Marsh Road, Naamans
  Creek, Walnut Lane,
  Lower Lane, Meadow
  Lane, Pond Road,
  and Sherwood Road
Arden, DE
www.ardenclub.com

The Villa
Avondale Avenue, North
  Hamlin Street, West
  Addison Avenue, North
  Pulaski Road
Chicago, IL

Meridian Park
  Historic District
34th Street, Washington
  Boulevard, 30th Street,
  Pennsylvania Street
Indianapolis, IN

Takoma Park, MD
Eastern Avenue, Sligo
  Creek Parkway, Takoma
  Avenue, and Elm Street

Takoma, Washington, D.C.
Georgia Avenue, Piney
  Branch Road, and Aspen,
  Fern, and 7th Streets, N.W.

Roycroft Community
Main and South Grove
  Streets
East Aurora, NY
716-655-0571
www.roycrofter.com

Byrdcliffe Art Colony
Upper Byrdcliffe Road
Woodstock, NY
914-679-2079
www.woodstockguild.org/
  white_pines.htm

Rose Valley
Rose Valley Road and
  Possum Hollow Road
Rose Valley, PA
http://w1.igateway.com/
  clients1/rosevalley/history.
  htm

Rosemont Historic District
Commonwealth Avenue,
  King Street,
  and Walnut Street
Alexandria, VA

Churches

SkyRose Chapel
Rose Hills Memorial Park
Whittier, CA 90601
562-699-0921

St. John's Episcopal Chapel
1490 Mark Thomas Drive
Monterey, CA 93940

First Church of Christ,
  Scientist
2619 Bowditch Street
Berkeley, CA 94704

First Unitarian Church
Dana Street and Bancroft
  Way
Berkeley, CA 94704

St. John's Presbyterian
  Church
2640 College Avenue
Berkeley, CA 94704

Swedenborgian Church
  of San Francisco
  (Church of the New
  Jerusalem)
2107 Lyon Street
San Francisco, CA 94115
415-346-6466

INDEX

239

Editorial Concept:
   Richard Olsen and Diane Maddex
Produced by Archetype Press, Inc.
Project Director: Diane Maddex
Designer: Robert L. Wiser
Editor: Gretchen Smith Mui
Research Assistant: Robert L. Maddex

Acknowledgments

A book like this is impossible without the help of friends, old and new. We thank the following: Margaret Adamic, Gregory and Kay Allen, Marcia Anderson, Allene Archibald, Giselle Arteaga-Johnson, Beverly A. Barnett, Arlene Baxter, Marion and Ted Binkley, Steven B. Blades, John Brinkmann and *American Bungalow,* David Cathers, Susan Cerny, Ann and André Chaves, Nick Clark, Robert Judson Clark, Patty Dean, J. Michael Dungan, Kathy Farretta, Jean France, Aaron and Sally Hamburger, Mr. and Mrs. James P. Harrison, Marka O. Hibbs, Monique Hoogenboom, Jennifer Johnson, Jody Jones, Paula Jones, Alan Jutsi, Wendy Kaplan, Ray and Shelly Kappe, Sandy Kennedy, Pamela D. Kingsbury, Don and Sally Kubly, Linda Lack, Richard Longstreth, Ann Scheid Lund, Alison Maddex, Tom and Beth Ann McPherson, William Marquand, Sheila Menzies, Kennon G. Miedema, David Mostardi, Elizabeth and Dennis O'Regan, Peter Olmsted, Thomas and Kathleen Plummer, Carol Polanskey, Alfred Pompper Jr., Morris Potter, Martin Ratliff, Julie Reiz, Mr. and Mrs. David Reynolds, Ann Richtarik, Cheryl Robertson, Cheryle Robertson, Jane S. Roos, Scott and Sallie Seltzer, Joanne Sklar, Carla Smith, Katie Somerville, Donald Songster, Joseph Taylor, Marilyn L. Thomas, Mr. and Mrs. Fairman Thompson, Nancy Townsend, and Randi Werner.

I also wish to acknowledge the Braun Library, Southwest Museum, Los Angeles; Clapp Library, Occidental College, Los Angeles; Historical Society of Southern California, Los Angeles; and all who made their sites available for photography. My typist and organizer, Marcie Chan, deserves special appreciation. The producer of this book, Diane Maddex, is a good friend who sees to it that things get done. Her editor, Gretchen Smith Mui, asks the right questions. And Robert Wiser must be the best book designer in the country.

Display Photographs

Page 1: The first issue of Gustav Stickley's *Craftsman* magazine. Pages 2–3: The Close, Short Hills, N.J. (see pages 128–33). Pages 4–5: Craftsman Farms, Parsippany, N.J. (see pages 64–71). Page 6: Ernest Batchelder bungalow (1909), Pasadena, Calif., now the home of Robert Winter. Page 7: Brandt-Serrurier House (1905, Greene and Greene), Altadena, Calif. Page 8: Fetcher House (1902, Augustus Higginson), Winnetka, Ill. Page 9: Hewitt House, Minneapolis (see pages 80–85). Page 10: Fonthill, Doylestown, Pa. (see pages 58–63). Page 11: Duncan-Irwin House, Pasadena, Calif. (see pages 38–49). Pages 12–13: Gamble House (1908, Greene and Greene), Pasadena, Calif. Pages 30–31: Craftsman Farms, Parsippany, N.J. (see pages 64–71). Pages 72–73: The Close, Short Hills, N.J. (see pages 128–33). Pages 134–35: Rose Valley, Pennsylvania (see pages 142–55). Pages 172–73: Mission Inn, Riverside, Calif. (see pages 174–81). Pages 204–5: Disney's Grand Californian Hotel, Anaheim, Calif. (see pages 226–33).

All photographs are by Alexander Vertikoff except as indicated below:

Page 1: *The Craftsman,* October 1901. Page 18: Martin Charles (bottom left); Robert Winter collection (top and bottom right). Page 19: *Craftsman Homes* (Stickley, 2d ed., 1909) (top); *The Craftsman,* January 1909 (bottom left and right). Page 21: Robert Winter collection (left); Los Angeles County Museum of Art, gift of Max Palevsky (center), photograph © 2003 Museum Associates/LACMA; Van Briggle Pottery (right). Page 22: Los Angeles Public Library. Page 23: Historic American Buildings Survey, Library of Congress (top); Greene and Greene Archives, Gamble House, USC (center); College of Environmental Design Documents Collection, University of California, Berkeley (bottom). Page 25: Robert Winter collection. Page 26: Frederick Law Olmsted National Historic Site, National Park Service. Page 27: Greene and Greene Archives, Gamble House, USC. Page 94: *Architect and Engineer,* Robert Judson Clark collection. Page 175: Mission Inn Museum (left and right).

Case binding ("Glenwood") and endpapers ("Birchwood Frieze") used courtesy Bradbury and Bradbury Wallpapers (www.Bradbury.com).

Photographs on pages 2–3, 8, 52–57, 72–73, 128–33, 140–41, and 226–33 used courtesy *American Bungalow* magazine.

Photographs of Fonthill used courtesy the Bucks County Historical Society.

Photographs of Craftsman Farms used courtesy The Craftsman Farms Foundation, Parsippany, N.J.

Photographs of Disney's Grand Californian Hotel used by permission from Disney Enterprises, Inc.

Library of Congress Cataloging-in-Publication Data

Winter, Robert M., 1924–
   Craftsman style / by Robert Winter; photography by Alexander Vertikoff. — 1st ed.
      p.   cm.
   ISBN 0-8109-4336-0 (alk. paper)
   1. Arts and crafts movement—United States. 2. Architecture, Domestic—United States. 3. Architecture—United States—20th century. I. Vertikoff, Alexander. II. Title.
   NA7208.W56   2004
   720'.973'09034—dc22

                                    2003021467

Compilation copyright © 2004 Archetype Press, Inc.
Text copyright © 2004 Robert Winter
Photographs copyright © 2004 Alexander Vertikoff
Published in 2004 by Harry N. Abrams, Incorporated, New York

Printed and bound in Singapore

10   9   8   7   6   5   4   3   2   1

This book was composed in Cloister Oldstyle (1913, Morris Fuller Benton) and Legacy Sans (1992, Ronald Arnholm), with display typography in Cloister Bold Tooled (1923, Intertype), all inspired by the late-fifteenth-century work in Venice of Nicholas Jenson, the first significant designer of a Roman typeface. William Morris admired Jenson's humanist-style design and in 1893 modeled his Golden Type for the Kelmscott Press on it. Other designers of the Arts and Crafts small press movement followed Morris's lead to create similar typefaces, paving the way for a general revival of interest in historic typography.

Harry N. Abrams, Inc.
100 Fifth Avenue
New York, N.Y. 10011
www.abramsbooks.com

Abrams is a subsidiary of